Proceed with Caution

A Diary Of
The First Year
At One Of
America's Largest,
Most Prestigious
Law Firms

William R. Keates, Esq.

HARCOURT BRACE LEGAL AND PROFESSIONAL PUBLICATIONS, INC.
Editorial Offices: 176 West Adams, Suite 2100, Chicago, IL 60603
Regional Offices: Chicago, Los Angeles, New York, Washington, D.C.

Distributed by:
HARCOURT BRACE AND COMPANY
6277 Sea Harbor Drive, Orlando, FL 32887
Phone: 1-800-787-8717
Fax: 1-800-433-6303

Requests for permission to make copies of any part of the work should be mailed to: Permissions Department, Harcourt Brace Legal and Professional Publications, Inc., 6277 Sea Harbor Drive, Orlando, Florida 32887-6777.

Printed in the United States of America.

DEDICATION

To my family and friends whose support never wavered.

INTRODUCTION

You don't know me, but you probably think you know people *like* me. As my first job out of law school, I was an attorney at one of the largest, most prestigious law firms in the country. For most law students, the job I had is considered a "dream" job, going only to the best and brightest law students. And to people outside the law, my job seems even more glamorous. Famous, blue-chip clients, huge paychecks, the prestige of being a big-time lawyer.

The truth is, after less than two years, I left the firm, burned out and completely dissatisfied with practicing law.

I became a lawyer probably for the same reason that most people do. Most of what I knew about lawyers was based on what I saw in the movies and on TV and read in books. I thought I knew what lawyers did. But lawyers in television programs like *L.A. Law* and *Perry Mason*, and books and movies like *To Kill A Mockingbird* and *The Firm*, create images of the lives of attorneys that are far from the truth. I know from personal experience just how harmful these misconceptions can be. They can lead people to choose a career in law which would ultimately make them unhappy.

It wasn't until I worked as a junior associate at an enormous law firm that I learned the truth behind the image. Some of what I'd believed *was* true—the money and the prestige of large-firm practice are undeniable. But the less savory aspects of the day-to-day life I led were completely unexpected. Because you now have my diary, you're better off than I was. Whether you're in college and considering law school, or in law school and considering pursuing a career at a large firm, or you're just curious what it's like to actually be what most people consider a "big-time" lawyer—now you'll know.

I wish *I'd* known.

Looking back, there are a number of myths I used to believe about practicing law. You may believe many of them yourself.

"Most lawyers prosecute or defend criminals."

Not true. Only 2% of practicing lawyers practice criminal law. In fact, many lawyers never even set foot in a courtroom!

"Lawyers are wealthy."

Wealth is relative. It's true that lawyers sometimes earn more than many people, but that increased income comes with a price: they often work harder, longer hours, and make greater sacrifices. In fact, you're probably much more likely to be able to make enough money to retire early from owning your own business than from practicing law.

"Being a lawyer is prestigious."

The public has a love-hate relationship with lawyers and the legal profession. On the one hand, in spite of well-publicized data about job dissatisfaction among lawyers, the public maintains a romanticized view of the legal profession: huge salaries, luxurious lifestyles, expensive possessions, high-profile cases. On the other hand, the legal profession is battling a severe image crisis: widespread public contempt. In polls of public opinion as to trustworthiness, lawyers frequently rank at or near the bottom, along with used car salesmen.

"The law requires novel and creative thinking."

Many people are attracted to practicing law because they think it will involve a real intellectual challenge. While it *does* require clear, logical thinking, most law practices *don't* require novel and creative thinking on a daily basis. In fact, many lawyers complain that the risks associated with departing from traditional, accepted principles actually *stifle* their creativity.

"Trying cases will be exciting."

Not true, because most cases never get to the trial stage. Instead, because trying a case is risky and expensive, more than 90% of civil suits—that is, suits between private parties, as opposed to criminal cases—end in settlement rather than trial. In fact, most courtroom lawyers (called "litigators") spend most of their time doing "pretrial" work, such as preparing motions, conducting discovery (finding out facts about the case from sources like witnesses and physical evidence), and engaging in settlement negotiations with the other side.

"International law is more exciting than domestic law."

A lot of people are drawn to the law because they want to be international lawyers, fantasizing about a life of travel to exotic places. The truth is most American lawyers who practice international law actually advise domestic and foreign clients about *American* law, particularly about importing and exporting goods to and from the U.S. That means their focus is more on *this* country's laws than on those of any other country.

"Practicing environmental law will help protect the environment."

Many a law student has been rudely awakened by the fact that much environmental law involves representing the interests of those who *harm* the environment. In fact, lawyers who litigate environmental law claims often focus more on cost-shifting than on protecting the environment. These cases typically revolve around who will be responsible for the cost of cleaning up a toxic site. Relatively few lawyers actually ensure compliance with environmental statutes and regulations on a full-time basis. A colleague of mine joked, "What do people think? A family of bunnies is going to hop into your office and say, 'Please protect my habitat?'"

"You can always leave the legal profession if you don't like being a lawyer."

In theory, of course, this is true, but many lawyers find themselves in a velvet trap. They'd *like* to leave the legal profession, but financial considerations stop them. Burdened with substantial debt from their legal education—many law students graduate facing student loan payments of up to $900 a month—they feel handcuffed to the profession, because they need a high salary to meet their financial obligations.

"You can do anything with a law degree."

Many college students go to law school to put off the "real world" for three years, believing that a law degree will give them a jumpstart in the business world. Not true! Lawyers are frequently surprised by the barriers they face when they try to leave the law and enter the business world. Most don't have the qualifications to enter business-related fields like marketing, advertising, accounting, finance, and communications.

What happens as a result of believing myths like these? All too often, top college students enroll in prestigious law schools as a next logical step toward success, at least as society defines success. Three years later, they graduate with substantial debt (as much as $90,000 at private institutions) and accept positions in the largest, most prestigious firms that make them an offer, only to discover that they don't like practicing law. But then, bound by financial considerations and loan repayment schedules, they're stuck. They *have* to stay in the profession. The naiveté of college and law school students with respect to the actual day-to-day practice of law isn't just a stage that's outgrown with experience. Instead, it lures thousands of people every year to choose a path that they may not otherwise have taken.

That's what happened to me, and many, many other people just like me. As a junior attorney with a large firm, I interviewed many law students who were just what I had been—uninformed about what practicing law at a large, prestigious law firm is actually like. One of the most common questions I heard was, "What do you do in a typical day?" This question reveals an unfortunate reality about the typical law school education: even though students learn about "the law," they don't learn about what it's like to *be* a lawyer. Most college and law students know woefully little about how law firms are structured, what typical work assignments are like, the necessity and impact of long hours, and the psychological and physical stresses of being a lawyer for a large firm. Based on myths they believe, they begin their legal practice terribly unprepared —as *I* was.

But I did something I don't think many other people do. I kept a diary. My diary provided a very necessary "release valve" for the pressure I was facing during the day. At work, I had to be orderly, focused, and logical in my writing. In my diary, I could pour out everything that was happening to me, in vivid, no-holds-barred terms. As you read the excerpts from my diary, I think you'll get a feel for what it's really like to lead the life I led. In the words of an old proverb, you'll have a chance to "walk a mile in my shoes." I've supplemented my diary with information gathered from other sources, including my colleagues, newspapers, and other periodicals. Was my experience typical of a large-firm associate? After reading every published source I could find about the practice of law, and speaking with hundreds of colleagues (and hearing about many more)—yes, I think it was.

Everything I describe in this book actually happened as I describe it. I have, however, made changes to names (including my own), locations, and descriptions of businesses to protect the identities of people, clients, entities, and their confidences. Any overlap between the names I've chosen and the real names of people or entities is purely coincidental.

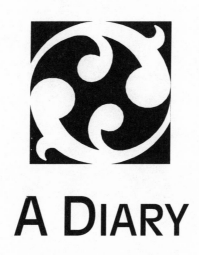

A DIARY

September 21

Today was my first day at work, my official entry into the practice of law.

Christine, the recruiting coordinator, told me to report to work at 9:30 a.m. I got there a few minutes early, about 9:25 a.m., feeling more like I was about to embark on another round of interviews rather than my legal career. While waiting for Christine in the firm's reception area, I realized that the firm has an incredible office—beautiful hardwood floors partly covered with intricate oriental rugs and complemented with contemporary artwork. At 9:30 a.m. sharp, Christine met me and walked me to my office, where I dropped off my coat and met my secretary, Nancy. Nancy is in her mid- to late-twenties and seems very professional.

Christine told me that the firm was going to have a "welcome" breakfast in my honor at 10 a.m. I thought it was a nice touch, but I really didn't feel like being the center of attention. We had some time to kill, so she brought me to her office and gave me a copy of the firm's office manual and a stack of paperwork to fill out.

When 10 o'clock rolled around, Christine stopped by my office to escort me to my breakfast. It was being held just off the lobby in the firm's main conference room, a spacious room with interior glass walls and a fantastic view of the city. Unfortunately, we were the first to arrive; the room was empty except for some muffins and bagels stacked on top of one another on a corner table. Christine and I made small talk and helped ourselves to a couple of muffins, pretending not to notice the conspicuous absence of my new colleagues. After a few awkward minutes, people slowly made their way in and introduced themselves to me. I was fairly nervous until *people started mingling with each other. After the breakfast, I went back to my office and settled in.*

About 2 hours later, Mike, a mid-level associate, took me to lunch at an Italian restaurant down the street. Mike was one of the people who interviewed me last fall. He's a seventh year associate, about 34, and seems to genuinely enjoy his job.

When we got back, I stopped at Christine's office again to see whether I was supposed to be doing anything in particular. She told me that she'd arranged for me to spend the afternoon meeting with the head of each administrative department so that I'd get to know my way around. With Christine at my side, I made the rounds: the mailroom, records, duplicating, word processing, and accounting. Then I went back to my office to take care of some paperwork before taking off about 6:30 p.m. It'll probably be the easiest day of my career.

Despite its uneventful nature, I'll remember today for a long time. In some ways, it's been my crowning achievement. As long as I can remember, I've been determined to become a top lawyer with unlimited career potential. Nothing was going to stop me from attaining my singular career goal. Through college and law school, I studied, memorized, and wrote until I was ready to drop. Today, I got the payoff, and it feels great. I'm now an associate at one of New York City's principal law firms and earning a salary I once dreamed about.

I'll be practicing law with the best of the best.

Ultimately, practicing law at a large firm made me miserable. But looking back, it's not hard to understand the career choice that I made—and why thousands of law students, like me, jump at the same chance every year.

Like most law students, I started taking a serious look at my career options in my second year of law school. That's when most law students look for a job, called a "clerkship," which is essentially a summer job between the second and third years of law school. These clerkships are very important, because for most students the ideal situation is to get an offer from the summer clerkship employer to come back after law school graduation as an attorney.

There are a variety of possible work environments, but they basically boil down to three basic choices: a large firm, versus a small or medium-sized firm, or the public sector. I *was* aware that working in the public sector or for a smaller firm offers a number of perceived benefits, including more relaxed work environments, smaller caseloads, more responsibility earlier on, and greater opportunity for advancement.

But as is true of many law students, I found the lure of working for a large firm too compelling to resist—huge salaries, prestigious credentials, famous clients and high-profile cases, and unparalleled resources. Whose head *wouldn't* be turned by perks like those? And although I quickly became dissatisfied with practicing law, there's no question that these benefits do exist. For instance, consider the financial rewards large firms offer. In John Grisham's novel, *The Firm,* Mitch McDeere was a first year associate at Bendini, Lambert & Locke, a law firm controlled by the Mafia. The firm enticed McDeere to join the firm with a financial package nothing short of amazing:

- ♦ a base salary of $80,000 for the first year, plus bonuses (and this was in Tennessee; an

equivalent salary in New York would be
$120,000).

♦ a low-interest mortgage to purchase a
home;

♦ two country club memberships; and

♦ a new BMW leased by the firm.

If you work for a firm *not* controlled by the Mafia, you'll
have to settle for a financial package that is not quite as
attractive as this.

But not by much.

Large firm salaries are exceptionally generous, especially compared to salaries paid by most nonlegal jobs. And of
the large firms, those located in New York City (called,
unsurprisingly, "New York firms") pay the most. In 1995,
most New York firms paid their new associates starting
salaries of $86,000; one even pays $90,000! Remember, this
is for people fresh out of school, with no practical experience, and frequently only twenty-five years old. These
firms also give staggering annual raises: second year
associates are paid between $86,000 and $102,000, while
third year associates are paid between $89,000 and
$117,000. (If you're curious, you'll find a list of salaries at
250 top law firms at the back of the book.)

That salary is even more generous if you do what some
new associates do and work for branch offices of New York
law firms. That's because some New York firms don't
adjust salaries downwards to reflect the lower cost of living
in the cities where branch offices are located. So, if you
work in one of these branch offices with an unadjusted
salary, you earn the same salary as associates in New York,
but have a much lower cost of living. With a few more
years' experience, the difference between these branch
office salaries and salaries for associates who work for local

firms can be enormous—as a fifth year associate, the difference can top $50,000 a year!

Salaries like these seem like manna from heaven when you compare them with the rather austere existence most law students enjoy. In fact, I've heard law school described as the last time poverty is fashionable. Once enormous paychecks start rolling in, *nobody* is at a loss to find ways to spend the money. I bought a Porsche. Other associates I knew lived in $1,500 a month apartments. It's just not too difficult to figure out how to drop huge sums of cash, once you've got the opportunity to do so.

In addition to new possessions, there are exotic vacations. And since large firms tend to be generous with vacation time—*paid* vacation time—new associates have both the means, and (at least in theory) 3 or 4 weeks off, per year, even in their first year.

Don't start salivating yet, though. Even though, on paper, new associates get upwards of a month's vacation time, few, if any, junior associates are actually able to take anywhere near that much time off. As we'll talk about a little later, the time pressure on junior attorneys is such that long vacations—and sometimes any vacation at all—are a pipe dream. The longest vacation I ever took was 5 days in a row. Most of the time, I took a day or two tacked onto a holiday weekend. While some other new associates took more vacation time than I did, there weren't many. And regardless of the time you take off as a new associate, you've got to be prepared to scuttle your plans on a moment's notice if a client emergency arises. So the 3 to 4 weeks' vacation looks much better on paper than in practice.

But despite the lack of vacation time, large firms offer many other benefits. On top of enormous starting salaries are generous benefits packages. Health, life, accident, and disability insurance, a 401(k) plan, parental leave (both paid and unpaid), bar association dues, and tuition and materials for continuing legal education classes—they're all standard. Some firms also provide dental insurance, and others match charitable contributions to associates' law schools. Most large firms also provide paid leave to study for the bar exam for new associates who start to work before they take the bar in July. They also reimburse the cost of bar exam review courses and bar exam fees (typically $1,500 or so), as well as reasonable relocation expenses.

What this adds up to is a financial package that few companies and businesses can touch. Whether the money is used to pay off law school debts or to buy "big ticket" items, like cars and homes, large firms provide a relatively carefree lifestyle—at least in terms of economics.

Like most law students, I often heard the arguments about the downside of high salaries at large firms—the most common one being that the return on the hours you work was actually lower at large firms because you had to work so many more hours than small-firm associates do. The theory is that although they pay less, small firms permit better lifestyles than large firms because they place a premium on quality of life issues like leisure time. My law school classmates and I were skeptical of these arguments, figuring that the substantial difference in salary— often $20,000 or more annually—more than made up for any increased workload, if indeed there *was* more work at large firms. I thought: I may work 10% harder than somebody at a small firm at first, but I'll earn at least 20% more than they will, so it's worth it. Ultimately, of course, I decided that it *wasn't* worth it, but there's logic to the argument nonetheless.

Money isn't the only reason people choose large law firms. For one thing, there's the prestige of being associated with law firms like mine. Working at a well-known, prestigious law firm with offices in major cities throughout the world offers credibility and credentials that can jump-start a legal career the way nothing else can. There's no question that experience with a "brand name" firm—one with international name recognition—makes finding another employer that much easier.

I was also conscious of the fact that if I didn't take a large firm offer right out of school, I might never get the opportunity to do so down the road. I had heard—and I still believe this is true—that it's a lot easier to move from a large firm to a small firm than to go the other way. That's because large firms traditionally prefer to hire graduating law students rather than associates from other law firms (who are called "lateral associates"). Even when they do hire associates from other firms, they normally choose them from other *large* firms, for predictable reasons—they are familiar with the environment, they're more likely to be comfortable and productive working for a large firm, and they'll have professional backgrounds that clients expect. The bottom line is that the decision to go to a small firm instead of a large one can have harsh, long-term financial consequences. Accepting a lower-paying position from the outset can leave you locked into a lower-paying career in the long run, by being forever frozen out of large firms. I didn't want that to happen me, so I grabbed the brass ring while I could.

On top of money and prestige, large firms offer the luster of working with famous clients, and handling high-profile cases. After all, since large law firms charge the highest fees, only the most well-heeled clients are able to afford them. Famous business executives, politicians, entertainers, and major corporations like Nike, Microsoft, and General Electric—these clients demand excellent legal representation, and are willing to pay handsomely for it. There's a definite cachet to representing clients who play a significant role in society and regularly make the newspapers and the evening news. When I was at the firm, I coveted those kinds of assignments. As you might expect, it doesn't take long at a large firm to view yourself as others view you: someone who's "made the big time." That was a feeling to treasure in light of the hard work and sacrifices that went along with it.

Another benefit to working at a large firm is less obvious to outsiders. It's the access to unmatched resources. One of the aspects of practicing law that's not attractive to most people is the research it entails. Representing clients virtually always involves researching cases and statutes to find the very best arguments to make on their behalf. That's especially true for new associates, who spend hour after hour in the library researching legal issues. Lawyers in solo practice or smaller firms often don't have the best resources at their fingertips, because the two main sources of legal research—extensive libraries and on-line databases—are too expensive for them.

Large firms, on the other hand, typically have the best resources available. Extensive libraries and well-qualified librarians are part of the trappings of large firms. On-line databases, like Lexis/Nexis and Westlaw, are probably the fastest, easiest, and most comprehensive sources of information lawyers have. They make it easy to find case law, statutes, law review articles, periodicals, news articles, government agency releases, and plenty of other information. They're updated all the time, and it's possible to do word searches to find information on them. As you might expect, this convenience comes at a price: on-line databases cost hundreds of dollars per hour. That puts them largely out of reach to all but the clients willing to pay high hourly fees—the kinds of clients large law firms have.

Another invaluable asset of large firms is the top-flight paralegals they employ. Paralegals are to lawyers what nurses are to doctors—they perform many of the more routine functions involved with the profession. Because large firms often handle very document-intensive cases, they typically employ more paralegals per attorney than smaller firms. For new associates like me, that meant I had subordinates from Day One to whom I could delegate tedious, time-consuming tasks. Without them, it would have been impossible to meet the strict deadlines I faced. Also, large-firm paralegals, like junior associates, accepted their jobs knowing they would regularly have to work long and unpredictable hours. Some paralegals even *prefer* working at large firms because of the opportunity to increase their income with overtime work. That was fine with me, because on the many days when I worked late and needed assistance, a competent paralegal willing to work overtime was greatly appreciated.

With considerations like these—great salary, excellent benefits, prestige, high-profile clients, unmatched resources—it's no surprise that students with the chance to join a large firm frequently jump at the chance.

Unfortunately, I had no idea what the downside of those benefits would be—what my day-to-day existence as a first year associate would be like.

I was soon to find out.

October 7

I got to work by about 9:30 a.m. today and put off work for a few minutes, eating my bagel and skimming the newspaper. I eventually settled in and forced myself to resume my research on the requirements for class action notice [that is, what kind of notification people need when they're "banded together" in a lawsuit because they have similar interests].

Ten minutes later, my phone rang—once—the dreaded internal ring. I hoped it would be Adam or Laura [fellow associates] calling to b.s. I answered it.

"Can you come in here?" It was Brad [my supervising partner] on his speakerphone. I barely got out the words "I'll be right in" before hearing the click of Brad hanging up. I grabbed a pad and walked to his office. I wondered if he wanted to talk about yesterday's conference call with the general counsel of Batton Utilities, a public utility holding company. Batton Utilities is contemplating submitting a proposal to the federal government in response to a shift of power among public utility holding companies.

Brad was working at his desk when I poked my head into his office. He was alone, so I walked in. I could tell by the way he looked up at me that he had twenty things on his mind.

Brad spoke quickly, as if we had been talking for the last couple of hours. He told me to prepare a memo to Batton Utilities' general counsel based on the legislative history of the Public Utility Holding Company Act of 1935—affectionately known as "PUHCA." He wanted me to find legislative history supporting Batton's arguments about PUHCA's legislative policy and its mandate for certain types of regulation of utilities.

Before yesterday, I had never heard of PUHCA. I didn't know what it did and had never seen it. Nonetheless, I knew I could handle legislative history. It's about as straightforward as it gets. But then Brad said, "Come back in the afternoon—early afternoon —and show me what you've found." At that moment, stress overcame me. What did he mean by "early afternoon"—12:30 p.m. or 3:00 p.m.? I didn't want to ask, but I also didn't want to report back to him two hours later than he was expecting. His vagueness was the last thing I wanted to deal with, particularly in light of my ignorance about PUHCA. In any event, I knew the next few hours would be a crazy rush, and that lunch had become a pipe dream.

I soon found the legislative history for PUHCA—a substantial amount of reading by any standard—and began skimming the text quickly, feeling like I was searching for two needles in a giant haystack. A few hours later, I had found a lot of material regarding PUHCA's mandate for certain types of utility regulation, but only minimal discussion of PUHCA's legislative policy. Unfortunately, I knew I had to start drafting something; Brad, the partner who hired me and with whom I expect to work closely in the future, had to have something to read soon. I drafted a quick and dirty memo to the client with the support that I had found. The memo had two sections, one for each of the two points Brad wanted me to research.

About 3:00 p.m., I walked into Brad's office to show him my memo. He was alone, and his spacious office was quiet. He looked up at me and said, "Good. C'mon in. Let's see what you found."

I walked over to him and put the memo in his outstretched hand. As he leafed through the pages, he seemed to ignore my explanation that there was little legislative history on PUHCA's *legislative policy. Then silence pervaded the room, disturbed only by the sound of pages being flipped. Finally, he broke the silence.*

"This is s**t, isn't it?"

The words seemed to reverberate throughout the room and inside my head. What did he mean? Did he mean my memo or the usefulness (or lack thereof) of PUHCA's legislative history to Batton Utilities? I knew I was going to have to guess—I didn't know him well enough yet to know what he meant. I had met him only a few times, and, before today, I had never worked directly for him.

Hoping he meant the latter, I responded rather sheepishly, "It's the best we have."

He didn't look at me or answer immediately. He just stared at my memo and kept flipping the pages. The silence was unbearable. Finally, he made an executive decision, and told me to "get rid of the first section" and send the rest to Batton Utilities.

I left Brad's office a little shell-shocked. I felt relieved because part of my memo was going to the client unedited, but I was reeling from my first one-on-one, hardcore experience with Brad—one of the biggest rainmakers [lawyers who lure and keep clients, and are considered very valuable as a result] in the firm.

I've thought a lot about what happened this afternoon, and I think I understand it now: Brad was just testing my mettle. To him, I'm just another "puppy" at the firm.

Making the jump from law school to practicing law was a shock to my system. By the time I got to the firm, I had spent three years intensely studying, memorizing, analyzing, and writing about the law. Yet, like so many first year associates before me, I found the transition to actually practicing law very difficult, personally and professionally.

Despite all my effort in school, I wasn't prepared for either the work or the psychological stress which made that period the most arduous and demanding year of my life.

This chasm between law school and practicing law isn't a new phenomenon; it's always existed. In law school, you learn to spot issues in complex fact patterns and analyze them, to invite rather than fear new ideas, and to examine and analyze the rationality of the rules and laws governing society. But that's got little to do with being a lawyer, and developing and maintaining a successful practice.

And the chasm between law school and the legal profession seems to be getting wider. Judge Harry Edwards of the United States Circuit Court of Appeals for the District of Columbia has said that "[w]hile the law schools are moving toward pure theory, the firms are moving towards pure commerce, and the middle ground—ethical practice—has been deserted by both." Abstract theory isn't much help to new associates trying to learn to manage cases and relate to clients, or to handle the routine aspects of practice like preparing privilege logs, interview memoranda, and witness preparation outlines. Law firms aren't much help in this regard, because teaching new associates these skills doesn't generate profits—the primary goal of many law firms.

Exploding technology makes the pressure on all lawyers, but especially new ones, even greater. Widespread computer use, high-speed copiers, fax machines, and online databases have quickened the pace of the practice of law, forcing attorneys to sift through ever greater amounts of information in shorter periods of time. That leaves even less time to acquire lawyering skills, which fledgling lawyers inevitably have to learn on the job.

Could this change? Sure. All kinds of people have proposed all kinds of solutions, but so far a lack of motivation has prevented any of them from taking a firm hold. Law firms could focus more on developing adequate associate training programs and improving work environments, and less on profits, although as businesses they're unlikely to do so. Law schools could expand their hands-on, clinical programs and externship programs to better prepare students for the "real world," and some have moved towards doing exactly that. Law schools could also move more toward a business school model by using a multi-faceted approach to problem-solving; for instance, law schools could use cases to teach students nonlegal solutions to problems. A school could have a corporate finance course that examines the legal, financial, accounting, and public relations problems associated with an actual merger. Or an administrative law course could examine an important social issue, like airline safety, and study how it's affected by governmental actions and the press. With this "real life" approach, law students would be better prepared for the practice of law *before* they actually practice it, and they'd be less stressed when they become lawyers.

As a new associate, I encountered this stress in a number of ways I never would have anticipated as a law student. I wasn't alone; most new associates experience the same feelings. One source of stress is discovering that law school leaves you woefully unprepared to actually practice law. As the author David Edelstein pointed out, most law students graduate eager to practice law. Their law school experiences have instilled in them a great sense of pride in their legal abilities: they respect the nation's legal system, see it as a potential vehicle of change, and are determined to pursue the idealistic goals their law schools encouraged. But as they plunge into the practice of law, they often change their views of the legal system, and sometimes become disillusioned with it. Many new attorneys, even if they performed well in law school, feel they lack the experience or knowledge to practice effectively.

The physical demands of practicing law are also a surprise. Law students often work hard, but no matter how diligent they were as students, they find that the demands of law school pale in comparison to the 60 to 100-hour weeks they regularly endure in practice. Within a few months of beginning their careers, new lawyers frequently see limits on the amount of work they can physically tolerate, which in turn limits their ability to practice law.

Learning about what it's really like to work with clients can also be extremely stressful. It's easy as a law student to envision working with clients in a friendly, thorough manner. After all, the only client contact many law students get is through law school clinics, which typically provide counseling to low-income clients or community organizations—both of which are grateful for any legal help they can get. There's a world of difference between these clients and the clients who pay big money for large law firms to represent them. The same student who just finished counseling a poor person in a dispute with their landlord will quickly find that providing legal assistance in a large law firm environment is completely foreign, since pressures and time constraints often lead to hurried and superficial client relations. In large firm practice, clients aren't viewed as a person or company in need; they are viewed as a continuing source of business in a highly competitive market. Clients know this, and the high legal fees large law firms charge make clients more demanding and increase their expectations. When the firms can't accommodate their requests, clients sometimes react with anger and disappointment. Worse yet, as a lawyer you sometimes find that there isn't much you can do to help your clients. The vision you once had of being a legal confidante to clients you know and trust may soon begin to crumble.

Another source of stress for new lawyers comes from learning to delegate work. For most of them, entering the legal profession is often the first time they are responsible for supervising *anybody*. As a law student I'd been used to doing all of my work myself. I never had to trust anybody else's judgment in performing tasks. But as a new lawyer, I had to delegate work, trust the people I delegated it to, and accept responsibility for projects that didn't proceed as planned—whether due to the faults of staff members or my own lack of supervisory skills.

Practicing law also creates stress since it frequently means a loss of the collegial spirit most of us enjoyed in law school. Although law school is competitive, most people enjoy an atmosphere of camaraderie and mutual support that's missing in practice. The pressures to succeed, competition to achieve partnership status, and intense time constraints leave most new lawyers with little opportunity to develop collegial bonds. As David Edelstein points out, the pressure to develop a self-reliant, "sink or swim" approach often leaves lawyers feeling lonely and isolated.

The personal sacrifices new lawyers make also contributes to their stress—although for many new lawyers, personal sacrifice is not a new experience. Most law students devote themselves single-mindedly to their studies. In fact, law school is often referred to as a jealous mistress, because of the stress it puts on relationships. As a result, many law students put off major life commitments like marriage and children, and postpone developing personal interests, hobbies, and pastimes. Contrast this with their peers who didn't go to law school, but instead cultivated full and well-rounded personal lives with meaningful interests and experiences in areas outside of work. David Edelstein points out that when new lawyers spend some of their few leisure moments with nonlawyer friends, they may recognize this disparity and feel the pressure to change to correct the imbalance in their lives.

New lawyers may feel even more lonely because they lose an old source of emotional and moral support—their families. I found, as many new lawyers do, that entering the legal profession creates the need for *more* support from family and friends. However, these very same people tend to view new lawyers as requiring *less* support, on account of their newly acquired privileged professional status. In the case of parents, their dependence on their child-slash-new-lawyer for legal advice and counsel leads to a reversal of the parent-child role. Being a counselor to the very people who once counseled you is a difficult transition to make.

Not surprisingly, all of these stresses can impact a new attorney's happiness. I found that while the transition into practicing law was difficult, it was eased by following a few simple guidelines. Among them were these:

First, I tried to emphasize quality over quantity. My firm, as with any firm, wanted to be sure that the legal advice it provided to clients was of the highest quality. As a result, firms seek associates who can analyze issues correctly and independently, and fully explore all relevant avenues. However, the temptation as a new associate is to rush through the first few assignments, in an attempt to seem efficient. I remember a summer associate who kept racing through assignments, hoping to impress the lawyers he was working for. His first two assignments were intended to last a week or more, yet he completed each of them in a single day! His third project was even larger, and should have taken 3 weeks to complete—yet he submitted his analysis after 3 days. At that point, one of my colleagues had to explain to him that the quality of his work mattered much more than how much he completed. Needless to say, I wasn't surprised when he wasn't invited back for a permanent position.

Second, I always tried to avoid asking questions when I could figure out the answers with a little research or independent footwork. Like other junior associates, I had to walk a fine line between clarifying assignments and relevant facts on the one hand, and seeming lazy or obtuse on the other. Once, shortly after I joined the firm, a senior partner asked me to research an issue for a meeting later that afternoon. Minutes after leaving his office, I realized that I didn't have a firm grasp of the issue he wanted researched. As I hastily began walking back to the partner's office, I mentioned to a mid-level associate working on the same case that I was going to ask the partner to clarify my assignment. The mid-level associate looked at me and said, "Are you sure you want to do that?" I knew immediately the answer was no; the partner was extremely busy with his own work and would only lose confidence in me if he had to explain the issue twice. I decided to review the materials I had again and, as I did many times thereafter, eventually figured out the issue on my own.

Third, I always tried to be as thorough as possible. It's just crucial to look at an assignment from every angle—to make sure that every research resource and case is current, to analyze alternative theories or approaches, and to provide a full answer to the legal issue being examined. Trust me—being thorough is a good preventative for sleepless nights.

This point was brought home to me while researching some new accounting standards for a senior partner at the firm. After finding certain accounting guidelines that seemed to apply to the facts at hand, I brought them into the partner's office and told him that I thought they were the right ones. He looked at them quickly and said that there were other standards that were more directly on point. He sent me back to the library with instructions to bring him a specific book containing the standards he had in mind. I went to the library, found the book, and returned to his office, where he was waiting to review it. He flipped through the table of contents, then the index, and then through a few pages. Finally, he found the page he was seeking, and said, "Ah, here it is. You know, there's a reason why we pay you young guys $90,000 a year. It's because we expect you to dig a little deeper." As it turned out, the provision he found was identical to the one I'd dug up; it just didn't seem that way to him because it was published in a very different format. But the experience revealed not only the firm's high expectations of my ability to research issues thoroughly, but also its belief that it was entitled to such thoroughness because it was paying top dollar for associates.

Fourth, I paid attention to every detail I could while working on my cases. I found that one of the most ironic facets of the law is that the correct answer to a problem often rests on small legal nuances and factual details. The presence or absence of a particular fact can frequently make or break a case. The senior attorney I worked for, Brad, was extremely adept at assimilating large amounts of information quickly, paying close attention to details, and using his mastery of them to weave brilliant defenses. His ability to identify the most critical of details while constructing solid defenses always impressed me, and I tried to emulate that particular skill.

Fifth, I was conscientious about creating good first impressions. As I later learned, lawyers who work with new summer and permanent associates virtually always form quick conclusions about them, and give "hallway evaluations" to other lawyers in the firm. I often heard about or participated in these hallway evaluations, and know that even one negative impression can have a devastating impact. In general, young attorneys who get a reputation for sloppy work—earned or unearned—have a very steep climb up the law firm ladder.

Sixth, I was vigilant about meeting deadlines, every time. This meant I had to carefully plan ahead, since partners, colleagues, clients, courts, and other parties often rely on assignments and legal services to be performed by a certain time. With the workload I had, and the interruptions I faced, of course this wasn't always possible, and in those situations I found the best route wasn't just to tough it out, but rather to let the supervising attorney know as early as possible if I couldn't meet a deadline.

I learned this lesson the hard way. My first assignment as a summer associate was to research whether we could squeeze one of our clients into an exception to a well-settled legal doctrine. The senior attorney who gave me the assignment asked me to research the issue and then get back to him by Friday afternoon. I just didn't feel comfortable with my research when Friday afternoon came around, and decided to buy some additional time by letting him contact me. He didn't try to reach me Friday afternoon, so I took advantage of that and submitted the assignment on Monday. The incident later came back to haunt me, though, because in his evaluation of my work for my mid-summer review, he mentioned that I didn't report to him by the established deadline.

I also quickly came to appreciate the importance of watching what's said around clients. When clients make unexpected requests for legal advice—as they often do—I learned that it was better to tell them I'd get back to them with an answer, and go away, research the question, and consult with a supervising attorney, rather than firing back an answer off-the-cuff.

A friend of mine at another firm told me a story that illustrates the risks of saying too much. It seems an insurance company had engaged my friend's California-based firm to help in defending against an environmental claim. This claim entailed reviewing huge volumes of documents in Arizona. So my friend's firm sent teams of associates to Arizona, all expenses paid, on a weekly basis. Because the insurance company also sent its own lawyers and paralegals, as did other insurance companies who were *also* defendants in the lawsuit, the document review facility was often staffed with numerous attorneys and paralegals from different firms. Associates were instructed not to discuss the case with anyone unless they knew with whom they were speaking.

After several months of document review, one associate from my friend's firm abandoned his professionalism and discretion when he began describing to a young woman who had recently arrived at the facility what boondoggles the weekly trips were. He talked at length about the free airfare, expensive meals, the easy work, and the evening partying the trips involved. As fate would have it, the young woman was a paralegal working for the insurance company—the client who was *paying* for all of his "perks" —and she promptly informed her superiors about his comments. Not surprisingly, the associate was fired before the end of the month.

My life as a new associate would have been a lot easier if I had delegated work more freely. I've mentioned the stress associated with delegating work, but the flip side of that was appreciating the importance of asking others for help rather than doing everything myself. I found that by delegating to paralegals and other staff members some of my more tedious assignments, I was free to do more interesting work.

I also wish I'd given myself greater latitude to make mistakes. As high achievers, law students often put enormous stress on themselves to be perfect, and I was no different. But as a new lawyer, I, of course, made mistakes; that's the inevitable result of inexperience. Rather than expect perfection and be inevitably disappointed, I'd have been better off to let myself be tripped up by inexperience—and focus, instead, on reducing mistakes caused by carelessness.

Finally, I tried to rely more on other associates within the firm for advice on assignments and office politics. When I learned to do this, I found that these insights gave me either the assurance that I was using the right approach, or guidance as to what the right approach might be. It didn't take me long to realize that getting the "inside scoop" on firm politics was crucial to my own political survival. Once I figured this out, I made sure I not only exchanged information with other junior associates, but I also went out of my way to gather key insights from mid-level and senior associates, who typically knew more about the latest political maneuverings and happenings. Such information enabled me to better understand the various personal agendas directing work flow and office decisions and, in turn, to better position myself with respect to issues and cases circulating in the office.

November 1

This entry is for the last 3 days—I've been working like a dog and haven't had the time or energy to make any entries.

The nightmare began on Monday morning, at a "welcome" breakfast for Rob, a new first year associate, in the main conference room. I was more than thrilled—a new, warm body to do some of the work. After mingling for a while, I wandered over to the corner and joined a small group of people talking to Rob.

As Rob and I were talking, Brad began moving towards the bagels and muffins and, coincidentally, towards our group. He broke into the group and started joking with Rob. Suddenly, Brad turned to me, as if I hadn't been there the moment before, and asked whether I was going to get Rob working on the brief with me.

Brief? What brief? I didn't have a clue as to what he was talking about, but I knew it was just a show for Rob's benefit, anyway. Hoping that a look of surprise didn't betray me, I told Brad I would if Rob was available to help out. As he began moving between me and Rob to get a muffin, Brad nodded confidently as if he had already established that Rob was firmly under his control.

After Brad was out of earshot, I asked whether anybody knew what brief he was talking about. No one knew. Brad has a tendency to assume that associates know all the developments in his cases even before he tells them. Little did I know what lay ahead of me.

By 11:00 a.m., I was in Brad's office with Dan [a partner] and Karen [a second year associate]. I learned that on Friday, the plaintiff in the Infomax case filed a motion to compel production of Infomax's director and officers' liability insurance policies. Infomax International is a computer database company that recently hired us. It's a shareholder derivative suit [a suit brought by shareholders to remedy a wrong allegedly done to the corporation, not to the shareholders themselves]—not the type of work I stay up late at night hoping to get. We represent Infomax, but we'll be reporting to the company's special litigation committee.

We've refused to produce the policies the plaintiff is seeking because, in our view, Infomax's insurance coverage has no bearing on the merits of the plaintiff's claims. Brad said that Karen and I were responsible for drafting a motion in opposition by Wednesday morning. As he was getting ready to leave for a business trip, he explained the general approach we should use and the types of arguments we should make in the motion. He then put on his coat and left the meeting, saying "Make it good. I want a power brief." The meeting was over by 11:15 a.m.

Karen and I began working immediately. It was tough going. We worked the next 15 hours without a break, leaving the office at 2:30 a.m. Tuesday morning. We had finished a first draft by then, but we both knew it was in bad shape.

As we agreed, we returned to the office by 9:00 a.m. to make sure we would finish in time. While we were editing and reworking the draft Tuesday morning, Brad called us from an airport and left a long voice mail message. He had apparently been thinking quite a bit about the brief and gave us new arguments he wanted to include in it.

We continued working through Tuesday and into the night. Fortunately, Tom, another second year associate, began helping us during the afternoon. His timing couldn't have been better—Karen and I were starting to get really irritable. But as the hours wore on, our fatigue grew worse. Karen had a little breakdown at about 1:00 a.m. this morning, but she recovered quickly and went right back to work. We finished the damn motion at about 4:30 a.m., and left copies for Brad and Dan to review before going home to crash.

By 11:00 a.m. today, feeling like the living dead, Karen and I dragged ourselves back to the office knowing full well that Brad and Dan would have comments and want us to rework our draft. We both looked and felt terrible. Thankfully, Dan edited most of the motion himself, taking some of the pressure off Karen and me.

By the time I left today, the end was in sight. We'll finish the motion tomorrow morning and then send it to our co-counsel for their review in the afternoon. We should be able to make the court's filing deadline no problem. It's been a rotten few days, though.

I worked in the litigation department at the firm. That is, my work centered around legal disputes. As this diary entry makes plain, a drawback of being a litigator is that your schedule is often at the mercy of courts and other parties. It's not unusual to get an assignment today, have a deadline that might as well be yesterday, and work until you drop to finish it. That's just one of the hazards of the specialty. They all have their pluses and minuses.

Exactly what will *you* do as an attorney? Most large law firms are divided into departments reflecting different specialties, like litigation, corporate, tax, trusts and estates, antitrust, and real estate, to name just a few. Law firms do this to organize their practices more efficiently, as well as to better meet the needs of their clients. When you join a large firm as a new associate, you'll either be asked which department you'd like to join, or you'll be assigned to a department. Some firms allow new associates to "rotate" through all of the departments before being asked to make a choice. Other firms ask new associates to specify their preferred departments, and then try to accommodate the preferences. Still others simply inform recruits when they make them an offer that the offer is good for a particular department.

By the way, once you're in a department—either by choice or not—you may have a tough time getting out of it. Most new associates who try to make a switch find themselves embroiled in firm politics, and answering to two departments for a while. Often it's actually easier to switch firms than it is to switch departments *within* a firm.

Of the different departments a large firm can have, the litigation and corporate departments are usually the biggest and most profitable. Here's the difference between the two: The litigation department's work usually revolves around a legal dispute, while the corporate department focuses on executing transactions or acquiring or selling rights. Predictably enough, lawyers who work in the litigation department are called litigators, and those in the corporate department are called corporate attorneys.

It's a mistake to think that just because large firms divide themselves into neat departments their cases must all fit neatly into one field of law. For example, corporate and litigation departments frequently have cases that overlap with the specialties of some other department at the firm. Let's say your firm has a case where its client company is being sold and there's litigation arising out of that sale. That case may implicate not just the corporate and litigation departments, but also the antitrust, tax, and real estate law departments. It may also be that your law firm gets a case involving a specialty for which it has no specific department. In that situation, the case would go to the department whose specialty most closely "fits" the case. So it's important to remember that these departmental splits are just a practical method of organizing expertise in the firm, rather than a set of rigid divisions.

As I mentioned, the corporate and litigation departments are typically the biggest and most profitable at large law firms. How do you decide which type of practice best suits you? Knowing a bit about what they do will help you choose.

Corporate attorneys are, broadly speaking, catalysts for business transactions. As a corporate attorney, you research the law, perform "due diligence" (that is, research the backgrounds of companies and parties before a transaction they're involved in is completed to check for legal or practical obstacles to the transaction), draft documents (like contracts, articles of incorporation, and stock offering documents), and help execute contracts and deals.

As an associate in the corporate department of a large firm, you'd prepare documents for transactions that your clients want to complete. For instance, a company planning to merge with another company might ask you to draft a merger agreement to protect the rights of both companies and their shareholders. Or an unincorporated entity (like a partnership) might ask you to prepare the documents necessary to make it into a corporation. Or a company might ask you to draft an employment and compensation agreement for its president.

If the idea of drafting these documents sounds intimidating, it shouldn't. Every large firm has an abundance of model or "form" documents you can refer to and emulate. For instance, if you're incorporating a client's business, you can turn to your firm's files for a model corporate charter and model corporate bylaws. You can "cut and paste" whatever sections are applicable, leaving you only to tailor the sections necessary to meet your client's specific needs.

While corporate attorneys are generally around before a transaction takes place, litigators generally jump into the fray afterwards, when some sort of legal dispute has arisen.

Simply put, as a litigator you fight your client's legal battles. You generally sue or defend parties in civil lawsuits or defend parties in government proceedings and investigations.

While the idea of being a litigator might bring to mind Perry Mason, as a junior associate in the litigation department of a large firm you'll do as much writing as your corporate counterparts. The documents you write will relate to the particular legal dispute that your client needs resolved. For instance, sometimes your clients will need you to prepare written "motions" on their behalf. Motions are oral or written requests to a court or judge to direct that some act be done in favor of the party making the motion. Some of the typical motions you might draft include motions to dismiss the case, motions to strike material from the other party's pleadings, and motions to suppress. You might also be called on to prepare a motion in opposition, if what your client wants to do is oppose a rule or order that they perform some act. Predictably, a motion in opposition sets forth arguments as to why the court should *not* direct that some act be done.

You'll also probably have to prepare legal briefs for your clients. A brief is a written statement arguing a case in court; it's a document any law student who's taken Moot Court, or any kind of mock trial course is intimately familiar with. In a brief you'd write for a client, you'd typically include a persuasive summary of relevant facts, you'd describe the applicable laws, and you'd give an argument showing why the law applies to the facts supporting your client's position.

Different "stages" through which cases pass will require you to write different kinds of briefs. At the trial level, briefs are submitted to the court just prior to trial and contain, among other things, a statement of the issues to be tried, a synopsis of the evidence and witnesses to be presented, and case and statutory authority supporting your firm's position at trial. If the losing party at the trial level wants to appeal that result, then the brief that goes to the appeals court is called an "appellate brief." That brief doesn't recount all the issues at the trial, but only the ones that attack or support the trial court's actions, depending on whether your client wants the trial court's decision overturned or affirmed.

Choosing a specialty is one of the most crucial decisions you can make as a new associate. Having said this, you might find it surprising to know that some lawyers never consciously choose a specialty. Many of the lawyers I worked with just "fell into" their specialties and wound up not liking what they got saddled with.

If your firm gives you a choice of departments, think carefully about which practice area will best suit your personality. Keep in mind that your specialty will affect not only the type of legal services you'll perform, but also the skills and knowledge that you'll develop. And it's important to remember that at a large firm, you'll likely only get one choice. There are very few attorneys at large firms who have more than one specialty, or change specialties down the road. As a result, the first choice you make is likely to affect the work you do for years to come.

If, for some reason, you get stuck with a specialty you don't like, make a change as soon as possible. The longer you wait, the harder it is to jump to another specialty. For one thing, as lawyers gain seniority, their firms may resist the change for fear of a loss of expertise that took the firm years to nurture and develop. Even if your firm does let you change specialties down the road, it may reduce your seniority or salary to reflect your newly acquired *inexperience* in your new practice area.

Changing specialties further on in your career can also impair your marketability in the legal community. After all, if you make a change when your salary has reached a high level, other firms who could hire you might choose not to, feeling they can get attorneys more experienced in the specialty for less money. Because your future potential in your *new* specialty is less valuable to a new employer than your past experience in your *old* specialty, it's very easy to get "pigeon-holed" in a particular practice area after just a few years in practice.

November 5

At about 3:30 today, Tara, a word processor, came into my office, visibly upset, and asked if we could talk for a few minutes. I told her we could, but she surprised me by closing the door behind her. A confidential discussion with one of the office's word processors? About what? She sat down in the chair opposite my desk and quickly collected her thoughts.

Tara told me that she had just been reviewed and that, during her review, the office manager told her that I had rated her poorly in her evaluation. She wanted to know exactly what she had done wrong that made me rate her poorly.

Caught by surprise, I looked at her blankly for a few seconds—I didn't even remember evaluating her at first. Then I remembered that a few weeks ago, I had evaluated each of the staff members on a work performance evaluation form. Tara was the only one I rated badly. On three consecutive occasions prior to the evaluation, I had to correct word processing mistakes she had made in my documents. When I got the opportunity to evaluate her, I rated her poorly, *hoping it might improve her future performance. I explained this to Tara, but she was still upset when she left my office.*

I'm still a little shocked over the whole incident. Having been at the firm only a few months, I didn't expect my evaluation to carry any weight. Hell, I'm still learning my *way around.*

I also can't believe that office management told *Tara that I was one of the attorneys that rated her poorly. Talk about a chilling effect on free speech! I thought office management would keep the evaluations confidential and use them to identify potential problems, not cause internal divisions between the staff and me.*

From this day forward, I'm going to write only good reviews and, if necessary, discuss problems with staff members privately.

There is a definite pecking order at large law firms, usually consisting of three layers: partners, associates, and staff members. Even though this hierarchy affects virtually every aspect of the firm, it is not commonly or even openly acknowledged by firm employees. Rather, it makes itself felt through established procedures, long-held assumptions, and implied messages and threats. There are well-defined authority figures and a clear chain of command. Everyone in the firm always knows exactly where they stand and from whom they should take orders.

How is the hierarchy structured? In the practice of law, a premium is placed on experience, which is considered the single most important factor in rendering sound legal advice. Accordingly, at the top of the hierarchy are the lawyers with the most experience—the partners.

There can be one or two levels of partners in a firm. If there's only one level, then all the partners are "equity partners." That means they share in the firm's profits and losses, and they are personally liable for the conduct of the firm and its attorneys. As a general rule, the partners with more seniority wield more power.

If a firm has two levels of partners, equity partners will be in the upper tier, and nonequity partners will be in the lower tier. As the name suggests, nonequity partners receive a salary rather than a percentage of the firm's profits. Typically, nonequity partners are made equity partners after several years.

One rung down the ladder from partners are salaried lawyers called "counsel" or "of counsel." These lawyers aren't really associates anymore but they aren't partners, either. Typically, firms give the "counsel" title to a lawyer whose experience and legal acumen they want to recognize, but for some reason don't want to invite to become a partner. Sometimes, for instance, the firm believes that it already has the right number of partners, or that adding a new partner wouldn't be fiscally sound. Other times, experienced lawyers from other law firms or the public sector are made counsel as a prelude to being invited to join the partnership. Most firms have relatively few lawyers serving as counsel in relation to the number of partners and associates.

The lowest ranking professionals in the firm are the associates, who are salaried employees of the firm. That's what I was. As with partners, there's a subhierarchy among associates based on seniority. Although that technically means that associates are subordinate to all associates with more seniority, in practice associates don't report to other associates who only outrank them by a year or two. Such seniority does come into play, however, when it comes to deciding who gets which office, and who gets to take part in external training sessions and/or seminars.

At the bottom of the law firm hierarchy are staff members. At a large firm, staff members include a whole army of people like office managers, paralegals, secretaries, word processors, librarians, proofreaders, accountants, recruiting coordinators, and computer management personnel. As nonprofessionals, they typically earn considerably less than the attorneys in the firm.

Of the staff members, a firm's office managers wield the most power and receive the highest salaries. They regularly meet with the firm's partners to discuss management issues like budgets, employment decisions, and staff compensation. Over time, their working relationship with the partners will imbue them with more power than their staff positions would otherwise carry—often giving them more power than many associates in the firm.

What ramifications does this hierarchy have on new associates? Being at the bottom of the pecking order, as a new associate you'll sometimes be frustrated in trying to complete your assignments on time. It's hard to be as efficient as senior attorneys because staff members will give your work lowest priority. When senior attorneys "bump" your work, it will seem as though you were unable to complete your assignments as quickly as expected—through no fault of your own.

To add insult to injury, some very experienced staff members, like career paralegals and secretaries of senior partners, frequently disregard the attorney status of new associates, and treat them with little respect. Even though you, as an attorney, technically outrank them, they will still try to steamroll you. And perhaps that's understandable, from the perspective that they've seen so many junior associates come and go over the years that they feel comfortable asserting themselves until you establish a place for yourself in the firm. From my own experience, I can tell you that it's wise to obtain solid footing in your firm before you challenge experienced staff members!

A lowly spot on the totem pole in the law firm also reflects itself in the kind of work assigned to new associates. Like other first year associates, I often found myself doing the "grunt work" in cases. Grunt work includes tasks like researching, drafting memoranda, reviewing documents, and preparing privilege logs. It makes sense from an economic standpoint to give this kind of work to new associates, in that it's unfair to expect clients to pay hundreds of dollars an hour to have a senior attorney do the routine kinds of tasks that a first year associate could perform in the same amount of time. But that's clearly not the only motivation. Since senior associates have all done their share of grunt work over the years, they've earned the right not to be burdened by boring and tedious work anymore. So there *is* a light at the end of the tunnel— although that seems like scant compensation when you're a bottom-feeding new associate trudging through a "document review."

November 10

I got on a plane to Miami today to work on my first document review.

Last week, the U.S. Attorney in Miami issued a document subpoena to Caltrex Corporation, our client, as part of a grand jury investigation. Mike, Peter [a second year associate], and I will be looking for responsive documents at Caltrex's headquarters so we can produce them to the U.S. Attorney's office.

I'm still kind of ambivalent about working on the case. Just about everybody says that document productions are boring as hell. We haven't reviewed any documents yet, but I'm hoping it won't be too bad.

On the other hand, this is my first business trip as an attorney. It definitely feels good to be out of the office and dealing with clients for a while—we spent most of today traveling and meeting Caltrex's corporate officials. It's certainly a nice change from sitting at my desk researching and writing memos all day.

November 13

Mike, Peter and I have been working closely with Terry, a 35-ish, mid-level manager at Caltrex, who knows where most of the relevant documents are located. It's pretty clear that Terry is high enough in the Caltrex hierarchy to know about the transactions under investigation, yet low enough to have to neglect his own work to help us. He's already complained twice about having to work late because of the time he's spent with us. The work itself—document review—is boring, and it seems to be getting worse each day.

Document reviews are the bane of a new associate's existence. First year associates are inevitably called on to pore through documents in connection with government investigations, or civil suits, or corporate transactions. These reviews consist of scrutinizing a sometimes towering collection of documents to determine the relevance and importance of each document in your case. Most new associates consider document reviews the worst and most undesirable assignments. Such reviews are virtually always tedious, boring, and completely unfulfilling intellectually. On top of that, a case might require you to pore over handwritten notes, memoranda, reports, and other documents hour after hour, sometimes for several weeks in a row. I had a friend who had to go through a roomful of records from a car dealership, looking for any evidence that the dealer had been unresponsive to complaints from customers. That meant going back through file cabinet after file cabinet of individual slips of paper, and reading each one carefully to see if it mentioned a customer complaint. Other document reviews require other kinds of searches. You might review documents to determine which ones are responsive to a government subpoena that your client received. Or to figure out whether your client ignored known risks before embarking on a project. Or to determine if your client's board of directors carefully considered a merger proposal before they voted on it.

Offhand this might not seem burdensome to you, but trust me, it is, due both to the volume of documents involved and the physical rigors of the task. Large firms often handle cases that call for tens or even hundreds of thousands of documents to be reviewed—in a single case! And it's not just a matter of reading the documents. There are the administrative hassles associated with collecting, reviewing, organizing, and shipping documents. With such huge volumes of documents involved, it's sometimes impractical to ship the documents to the law firm. And that means attorneys and paralegals have to travel to the documents. So you trudge out to a client's office or, more likely, storage facility, and work with the client's legal department and/or corporate officials and employees to figure out where relevant documents might be located. This task is sometimes like finding a needle in a haystack, and it's made even more difficult by a kind of Murphy's law: the most important documents always seem to find their way into the most unlikely files.

Actually reviewing documents themselves sounds like simple paper-shuffling, but in fact it's exhausting, both mentally and physically. You have to carefully examine each potentially relevant document, even if that means rummaging through paper for hours or days without finding anything really significant. Oftentimes you never find the kind of document you're seeking. That's a disappointment if you're looking for "helpful" documents—ones that will get your client off the hook—but a relief if you were searching for "damaging" papers, like ones indicating fraudulent conduct. Document reviews may also require you to index, copy, and ship relevant documents back to the office, where they can be further reviewed and processed.

As the most junior attorney on a document review, you'll typically be called on to prepare a memorandum documenting the search. This memo describes the steps you and your colleagues took to ensure a thorough search and review of the documents, and it's designed to protect the firm from any challenge to the search methodology, whether that challenge is from the client, opposing counsel, or the government.

The most junior attorney on a document review also usually winds up preparing the "privilege log." I've included a page of a privilege log on pages 38–39, so you can see what one looks like.

A privilege log arises in situations where your firm is reviewing the documents in order to produce them to a party on the other side of a case, and there's a possibility that the documents in question might be protected by the attorney-client privilege, the work-product doctrine, or any other privilege. (Privileges protect parties from having to reveal confidential communications so as to encourage them to speak freely. The work-product doctrine basically means that the other side in a case doesn't have access to the work you've done for *your* client.) Obviously, if you're handing over documents to the other side in a dispute,

EXAMPLE OF A PAGE FROM A PRIVILEGE LOG

Date	To	From	CC	Description	Grounds for Privilege
6/8/94	P. Roberts	Outside Counsel, J. Smith	A. Lithe	Letter regarding conference with S. Boyd	Attorney/Client
6/14/94	Outside Counsel, R. Giles	B. Hill		Letter regarding status of internal investigation	Attorney/Client
6/21/94	P. Kelly	Outside Counsel, R. Giles		Memorandum regarding telephone conference with L. Lappert	Attorney/Client; Work-Product
6/30/94	T. Keller	Outside Counsel, J. Smith	P. Roberts	Letter regarding employment of compliance officer	Attorney/Client
7/16/94	Outside Counsel, B. Cohen	P. Roberts		Letter regarding October 3, 1994 deposition	Attorney/Client

7/25/94	T. Keller	Outside Counsel, B. Cohen		Memorandum regarding research conducted in connection with internal investigation	Attorney/Client; Work-Product
8/6/94	B. Wilks	Outside Counsel, G. Cohen	P. Roberts, B. Hill, T. Keller	Letter regarding production of documents to the United States Securities and Exchange Commission	Attorney/Client
8/14/94	Outside Counsel, J. Smith	K. Collins		Letter regarding termination of employment of corporate officer	Attorney/Client
8/21/94	H. Frank	Outside Counsel, M. Barry		Memorandum regarding internal investigation with Counsel's handwritten notes	Attorney/Client; Work-Product

you're not going to want to give them anything more than they're entitled to—so it's crucial to separate privileged documents (which don't have to be turned over) from non-privileged documents (which do). It's so important, in fact, that attorneys typically go through documents a second time just to make sure no privileged documents were overlooked. Once privileged documents are identified and set aside, a junior attorney prepares the "privilege log," noting the privileged documents.

The whole document review process doesn't sound very exciting, does it? It's not, and that's why document reviews are so dreaded by new associates. But they *do* have a bright side. For one thing, a document review may be one of the first assignments that gives you significant client contact and responsibility. Instead of sitting behind your desk or in the firm library reading and writing memoranda, you actually get to go out and see clients. It's not very "sexy" client contact, but it does give you a good opportunity to develop your client relations skills. Also, if each attorney on the reviewing team is responsible for a certain distinct aspect of the review (which frequently happens), you may have more autonomy in handling your work than you normally do.

There's also a certain satisfaction you can get from knowing that document reviews are a critical part of any case. Any subsequent work on the case relies on a full understanding of any underlying, relevant documents. They help support positions and arguments that your firm will take in the case, and they have a lot more credibility than witnesses with fading memories or questionable personal motives. And even though a document review is a constant reminder of your junior status in the firm, you can console yourself with the fact that *every* attorney who works on the case will, at some point, have to review and

gain a working knowledge of all of the important documents in the case.

November 20

*Today, Brad, Jack [a partner], Dan, Mike, Karen, and I met in
the main conference room to figure out what has to be done in the
Infomax case. We divided up the work and then assigned deadlines
to the extent we could. I didn't say much during the meeting—I
just hoped I wouldn't get dumped on too badly.*

*For the time being, my main assignment is to research and
prepare a memo on Infomax's ability under Delaware law to
indemnify its directors for legal expenses and fines that they might
have to pay if they're found liable. The memo should take a few
days, at least. I'll have to research Delaware law on indemnification
and then analyze Infomax's charter, bylaws, and indemnification
agreements with its directors to see whether they have any indemnification provisions.*

*I don't think the assignment will be too bad. It could've been
worse—Karen got stuck with a memo comparing and contrasting
the provisions of Infomax's six directors' and officers' liability
insurance policies.*

Do you like libraries? Have you ever been in a law
library? If you aren't in law school, seek out a law school or
public law library, and spend an hour there just looking
over the kinds of books it houses and the various subject
matters of the books. It doesn't matter if you don't understand the jargon; you're just looking to see whether some
of the subjects interest you, and whether you'd want to

spend a good part of your day with those subjects and those books. Because as a junior associate in a large law firm, that's what you'd spend the bulk of your time doing.

The amount of time you can expect to spend in the library makes it crucial that you be the kind of person who would enjoy—or at least, be able to bear—doing a lot of research. Look at your own background. When you chose your college classes, did you avoid courses that required a research paper, believing that exams were much less work? Or did you prefer classes with research papers, feeling that you'd rather have the opportunity to dedicate the time and effort necessary to get a good grade on a paper rather than risk everything on a one-shot, timed test? If you preferred classes with exams, ask yourself whether you want to spend much of your time doing something you strenuously avoided as a college student. On the other hand, if you preferred classes with research papers, you'll more likely be happy as a legal researcher during your first year at a large law firm.

If you're not in law school, you might have a hard time understanding exactly what "legal research" is. You might think, "What's the big deal about getting out a legal encyclopedia and looking up what the rules are?" Unfortunately, that's not the way it works. Instead, as the popular legal writer Christina Kunz points out, "The law does not come wrapped in a tidy, clearly labeled package. Discerning what the law is requires gathering bits and pieces from a variety of sources, sorting them according to their relative weights and relevance . . . and combining them into as cohesive an analysis as possible."

So, as a junior associate you'll spend the bulk of your time gathering those "bits and pieces" for your supervising attorney(s). Ideally, you'll find "primary" authorities for your client's position. Those include sources like constitu-

tions, statutes, charters, ordinances, and judicial cases—
that is, any statement of the law issued by a governmental
body acting in its law-making capacity. As a researcher,
you "strike gold" when you find a primary authority to
support your client's position. If you're not so lucky, there
are always so-called "secondary" authorities you can use.
Those include sources that are persuasive, like dictionaries,
treatises, encyclopedias, legal periodicals, restatements,
and uniform and model statutes. If you use these kinds of
resources when you first start to research an issue, you'll
find that they frequently point you to more desirable
primary sources.

What do you do with the information you gather in
your research? Sometimes a supervising attorney will just
ask you what your research turned up. But that's not likely.
Instead, supervising attorneys will probably ask you for a
"legal memorandum" on a particular issue confronting one
of your clients. Legal memos are designed to identify the
legal principles that govern particular issues raised by
cases, and apply those principles to specific fact situations.
They shouldn't present arguments only for your client, but
should, instead, objectively analyze the legal issues and
facts and weigh the strengths and weaknesses of each
party's arguments. For instance, let's say that you had a
client who was trying to argue that she was a party to a
common law marriage, and deserved a property settlement
from her "husband" as a result. A legal memo you wrote
would cover your state's position on common law marriage, what elements would go into creating a common law
marriage, and what elements are present in your client's
case. It wouldn't do what a legal brief for your client would
do, and argue that there *was* a common law marriage.

As a junior associate you'll find that a legal memorandum will always take longer to write than you originally

anticipated. It simply takes time to ensure that you've stated all of the relevant law clearly and accurately, and applied that law to the facts of your particular case, without showing a bias toward any party. You'll find that once you've finished a first draft of the memo, you'll want to revise it and edit it to devise better ways to express and organize your ideas. Another thing that consumes time in writing legal memos is that the way sources are cited is very precise. If you aren't in law school, it may seem to you that as long as the attorney who's reading your memo can identify which case you're talking about, that's all that should count. Unfortunately, that's not the way it is. Every underline, every parenthesis, every comma, dot, and space has to be precise. It may seem unbelievable, but attorneys take these case citations very seriously—and so you should, too.

Even though legal memos are routine assignments, it's a mistake to take them lightly. They can help you—and hurt you—in a number of ways.

The most obvious benefit from writing legal memoranda, and doing the research that goes into writing them, is that you learn about various bodies of law. You'll be surprised how much law you'll remember from your research assignments and apply to similar fact patterns that arise in future. Legal research also helps you to "think like a lawyer"; that is, to think in a logical, focused manner about a particular issue. I've always likened research assignments to puzzles that challenge you to assimilate and express the law logically and cohesively.

Another clear benefit of writing legal memoranda is that when it comes to learning how to write well, nothing beats practice. As a junior associate you'll find that over time, you'll learn to draft memoranda that present logical, clear analyses of even the most complicated legal issues.

Writing legal memoranda also gives you a sense of autonomy that's otherwise hard to come by as a new associate. Researching issues and preparing your analysis of a complex legal issue is typically something you'll do alone. Ordinarily, once you get a research assignment, you'll be able to complete the assignment any way you want within a given period of time.

That's not to say that research assignments and legal memoranda aren't without their drawbacks. For one thing, many of them are boring. No matter how eager you are, it's really hard to muster enthusiasm to research the law governing the sale of whole-life insurance, or the indemnification of corporate directors. And even if you initially find an assignment interesting, your interest will often fade once you've solved the research "puzzle," and figured out what the answer will be. Once you've conquered the challenge of the issue posed to you, you'd much rather move onto a new assignment. Instead, you'll have to spend hours, days, or weeks preparing a written analysis of your answer, with correct citations, in a formal legal memorandum.

Interestingly enough, even though you do legal research largely on your own, you'll find that research assignments can be very stressful—especially if you're working on a tight deadline. It's enough to set your hair on end, knowing that if you accidentally miss something important in your research, you may face disciplinary action from your firm or bar association, you'll anger clients, and, in extreme cases, you may leave yourself and your supervising attorney open to a legal malpractice suit. Even if you think you've identified and examined all of the relevant primary and secondary authorities, you'll still inevitably question your research skills, and have panicky moments over the accuracy and completeness of your research. For instance, what if your supervising attorney asks you to find support for a legal proposition that, unbeknownst to him or her, doesn't exist in your state?

One of my friends at another large firm was asked to research an issue involving contracts. It seems a very wealthy client wanted to get out of a provision in a 3-year-old divorce agreement in which he'd agreed to set up an $8,000,000 trust fund for one of his children. Her supervising attorney insisted that he had seen case law supporting the client's ability to wriggle out of this provision, although he couldn't remember the name of the case. She spent 27 consecutive hours in the firm's library, searching in vain for any case supporting the proposition. As it turned out, the supervising attorney had misread the case in question; it didn't stand for that proposition at all, and in fact there *was* no case law to support the argument he wanted to make. But in the meantime, she was under intense pressure and faced the wrath of the supervising attorney. No matter how meticulous your research is, it takes enormous confidence to overcome nagging doubts that you simply failed to find the relevant case law or statute before you are prepared to explain, in writing, that it doesn't exist in the state.

If worse comes to worst and it turns out that you make a significant mistake in a legal memo, you're faced with the prospect of that very memo being used as "Exhibit A" when it comes time for your performance evaluation at the firm. Realizing that your memorandum contains a mistake after you submit it to a partner will make your stomach drop, and you'll do almost anything you can to get the memo back before (s)he reads it.

December 8

Today, I found out I'm heading back to Miami.

Peter was walking back to his office with a cup of java when he stopped by my office. He's a nice guy, but we don't have enough in common to socialize outside the office. Even in the office, we usually talk only about the Caltrex case. When he poked his head in my office, I was pretty sure it was work-related.

Entering my office, Peter asked me whether I had heard the news. Without waiting for a response, he said that Caltrex had just gotten another subpoena—an even broader one—from the U.S. Attorney's office in <u>Texas</u>.

Peter droned on, but I stopped listening. I was reeling from the thought that Mike, Peter, and I would be sent to Miami again to respond to the new subpoena. I knew there was no good reason not to send the same team. The reality is that we work fairly well together, and we're already familiar with Caltrex's corporate personnel and documents.

But I'm frustrated. The new subpoena—from a different U.S. Attorney's office—means another couple of weeks of document review, essentially doing the same drill all over again. I'm so damn sick of reviewing documents. I didn't go to law school for 3 years to review documents.

As a junior associate in a large firm, you never handle projects all by yourself. I was always working with at least one supervising attorney and frequently with teams of other associates, because the cases we worked on were too big for just a couple of lawyers to handle.

When your firm gets a new case, the first thing it will do is assign lawyers and paralegals to work on it. Intuitively, this may not seem like a big deal. But, in fact, your firm's philosophy and practices with respect to staffing cases will have a huge impact on the quality of your life, in *and* outside of work.

The same hierarchy that works in a large firm itself also applies to the staffing of any particular case. In a large firm, as I've already mentioned, first year associates are the bottom-feeders; counsel, mid-level, and senior associates are on the middle rung; and partners are at the top. In individual cases, law firms mirror this structure by, in effect, creating numerous subhierarchies to meet the staffing requirements of each case they handle.

As you might expect, a partner or senior associate is normally in charge of a case, and (s)he will manage the case and communicate regularly with the client. Usually, attorneys manage the cases they bring to the firm. However, if they don't have time for that, they'll delegate the management function to another partner or to a senior associate.

Of course, the number of attorneys assigned to any given case depends on the size of the case. Small cases typically only need two attorneys: a supervising attorney and a junior associate. If you're a junior associate on a small case, you'll find that the downside is that you'll do a greater percentage of the work. However, a benefit is that working on a small case is often more rewarding and educational than working on a large case. Why? In a small case, you'll be able to see the "big picture" and perhaps participate in planning overall case strategy. You'll get valuable exposure to clients. And you'll get the chance to work directly with a partner or senior associate, and learn case management skills. Most junior associates find that the insights and lawyering skills of more senior attorneys are among the most valuable resources a large firm has, and small cases give you a great opportunity to draw on that resource.

For all of their benefits, small cases are the exception rather than the rule at large firms. That means that there are surprisingly few opportunities to work closely with partners. In fact, large-firm associates commonly complain that they have little or no contact with partners, who are rarely available for advice or input.

Much more common at big firms are large, complex cases. These cases require a supervising attorney, at least one mid-level associate, as well as several junior associates. The mid-level associate's role is to bridge the gap between the junior associates and the senior attorney. With their greater experience, mid-level associates can discuss overall case strategy with the supervising attorney and then decide how to delegate work to the junior associates on the case. That frees up supervising attorneys from routine case management so they can focus on issues that require their expertise.

Regardless of the size of the case, a firm's philosophy on case staffing will have an impact on how many attorneys are assigned to any given case. And that, in turn, can have a direct effect on the number of hours you, as a junior associate, will have to work. Some firms are known as being "lean and mean" in their case staffing because they routinely assign as few lawyers as possible to a case. As you can imagine, although this means longer hours, it also brings greater responsibility, which is hard to come by for most junior associates.

Other firms prefer a team approach, assigning more attorneys to a case to work simultaneously on different parts of the case, in isolation. While this gives the firm more flexibility in managing cases, it reduces the amount of responsibility each junior associate receives—and makes the assignment correspondingly less rewarding. My firm generally embraced the team approach for its large and/or important cases, of which it had many. I worked on several cases staffed with a senior partner, junior partner, mid-level associate, and one or more junior associates.

Firms differ not only in how they staff particular cases, but also in the way they assign individual attorneys to cases over time. You may find that your firm staffs cases so that the same group of lawyers works as a team on every case. When this happens it's typically because a partner or senior associate believes the team of lawyers works well together, and has the clout to see that the team stays together. If you're a member of such a team and you actually do work well with the others, then you're much more likely to enjoy your work and learn more from senior lawyers on the team. But if you don't like the team, watch out—you'll find it difficult to get off the team without stepping through a minefield of career-jeopardizing office politics.

Another downside of the team approach is that there may be a conflict between the schedules of your senior attorneys and you. If the senior attorneys on the team prefer to stay late and work late, you'll have to match your schedule to theirs. If they like to work early and leave early, you'll be expected to do the same—because if work schedule differences arise, they'll be resolved in favor of the more senior attorneys, not you.

December 13

This afternoon, Tommy, one of the mailroom clerks, dropped off my "Attorney/Client Workload Summary" for November. I billed 191 hours and had 3 nonbillable hours.

I'm definitely relieved about my billables—everybody seems obsessed with billing hours, and I really wasn't sure whether I was billing enough. If I were to bill 191 hours every month, I'd bill just under 2,300 hours for the year. That should be more than enough—the firm average is a little over 2,000. But even if it's not, how can they blame me for low hours as long as I do all the work they give me?

The concept of "billable hours" permeates virtually every aspect of law firm life. You undoubtedly already know that lawyers bill by the hour—but without living under the hourly system, it's hard to understand why law firms use it, and the dramatic impact it has on you when you work for a law firm.

At the outset it's important to appreciate that at their core, law firms are businesses like any other. That is, their aim is to make a profit. They do so by providing something the marketplace demands, just like your corner drugstore, or General Motors. However, as a service-provider, they're providing a service as opposed to a product. Some law firms have become even more like companies by dissolving their partnerships and forming corporations instead, in order to limit potential liability. And many firms now even have their own marketing or public relations departments!

Like every business, a law firm maximizes its profits by increasing its income and minimizing its expenses. The firm's income comes from increasing the number of hours and services it provides, either by increasing its client base or performing more services for the clients it already has. At the same time, it will seek to reduce its expenses by limiting the amount that it pays to provide its services and reducing inefficiencies.

When you think about it, there are a number of ways law firms could determine how much to charge their clients without having to resort to billing by the hour. For instance, they could come up with a "shopping list" of prices for handling certain kinds of transactions. Or they could offer to work for a fixed price up front for each case, deal, or project they handle. But that's not how most law firms work. Instead, they typically bill their clients according to the number of hours their lawyers and paralegals spend working on particular matters. These hours charged to clients are commonly called "billable hours." They're called that because they consist of hours spent on work pertaining directly to a client's case, whether it's researching, negotiating, litigating, or any of a thousand other services a client's interests may require. Contrast those with "nonbillable hours," which refer to time spent on anything that *doesn't* pertain directly to a client's case and thus *can't* be charged to a client. Nonbillable matters include things like office administration, interviewing potential lawyers for the firm, taking part in continuing legal education programs, training, and pro bono cases (that is, representing, at no-charge, those who need legal help but can't afford it).

You can immediately see the kind of incentives the hourly system creates. Because a law firm's revenues correspond directly to the number of hours it can bill to clients, it will be attracted to complex, time-consuming cases. You might also expect law firms to encourage their associates to draw out assignments as long as possible, so as to squeeze as many billable hours out of each assignment as they possibly can. That doesn't happen largely because encouragement like this would clearly violate ethical guidelines and professional standards. Instead, I found that I was encouraged to bill the exact amount of time I spent completing any particular assignment, even if I believed, in hindsight, that I could have been more efficient. Of course, the hours *I* recorded as being billable hours didn't necessarily translate into billable hours to the firm's clients. Instead, partners in the firm used their greater expertise to determine how much of each associate's time should actually be billed to the client. For instance, a partner might have decided it was appropriate to bill a client for all 9 hours I spent on an assignment (at my billable rate of $150) if the same task would have taken her 3 hours (at her billable rate of $450). That meant the cost to the client was $1,350 regardless of whether I did the work or the partner did the work, consistent with the theory that an attorney's hourly rate reflects his or her efficiency and experience. A new associate's hourly rate usually tops only that of paralegals and other staff members in the firm, but increases with experience.

Even though associates are not encouraged to prolong their assignments, the hourly system *does* seriously impact their quality of life. That's because the more work the firm can squeeze out of them, the more profitable the firm will be. I've mentioned before that associates are paid on a salary basis—a very *generous* salary, but a salary nonetheless. And the firm has to pay that salary regardless of how many billable hours its associates work. That makes firms very conscious of how many billable hours their associates rack up. Some firms translate this vigilance into a minimum number of billable hours their associates must work on an annual basis, typically around 2,000 hours. (They may also have an additional requirement for nonbillable work, like recruiting new associates and writing articles.) The firms that don't have these annual minimums don't typically require their associates to work fewer hours, by any means. In fact, firms whose services are in high demand—or those functioning as modern-day "sweat-shops"—are not likely to have minimum billable hour requirements at all. For these firms, the caseload is so heavy that associates routinely bill many more hours than are necessary to make the firm profitable.

Regardless of whether a firm has a minimum annual billable hours requirement or not, junior attorneys are constantly reminded that the firm is aware of their billable and nonbillable hours. They typically do that by way of individualized monthly summaries of billable and non-billable hours for the prior month and from the beginning of the year, so that attorneys know where they stand. On the next page is an example of an attorney workload summary.

When we're talking about billable hours, it's crucial to remember that billable hours bear little resemblance to the hours you actually work. It's easy to slip into the trap of thinking, "If I've got to bill 8 hours a day, I can figure in an hour for lunch, and that means I'll be working 9 hours a day altogether. That's not so bad." The problem is, that's not realistic. It's simply not possible to bill every minute at the office. Apart from lunch, time spent switching between projects and taking inevitable breaks all eat a chunk of time every day that's not billable to any client.

As a rule of thumb, it takes between 9 and 11 hours to bill 8 hours. I found I spent 10 hours for every 8 I billed. Surveys of large firms have shown that associates regularly work about 10% more hours than they bill. So, to bill 2,000

Attorney Workload Summary

Matter	5/1 to 5/31 Hours	1/1 to 5/31 Hours
18785 Resources Unlimited, Inc.		
18785-1000 General	0	9
18785-1002 Audit Report	46	191
TOTAL CLIENT	46	200
19978 Computer Technologies, Ltd.		
19978-1001 Class Action	12	103
19467 GHT Enterprises, Inc.		
19467-1000 General	23	90
19888 General Systems Corp.		
19888-1004 Compliance Review	48	77
19976 First Bank of New York		
19976-1000 General	12	167
19976-1001 SEC Inquiry	0	110
TOTAL CLIENT	12	277
19917 Arcco Industries, Inc.		
19917-1000 General	14	88
18876 HomeBuilders Corporation		
18876-1001 Grand Jury	22	122
99999 Office Administration		
99999-2000 Recruiting	1	6
99999-2200 Vacation	2	4
99999-2400 Illness Absences	0	2
TOTAL CLIENT	3	12
Billable:	182	957
Pro Bono:	0	0
Firm:	3	12
TOTAL	185	969

hours a year, an associate at those firms would have to work an additional 200 or so hours—an additional *five* 40-hour workweeks!

If you travel frequently on business, the load is a little less cumbersome for a couple of reasons. First, I found that while traveling and focusing on one client's work I had fewer distractions than I did at the office. Also, time spent traveling is billable, even if you're sleeping on the plane or train. These "soft" billable hours let you bill time when you're not "working" in the true sense of the word, on the theory that if you were at the office you'd be doing work for other clients and billing them.

No matter how my billable hours were amassed, whether at the office or on the road, I found myself envious of my public sector counterparts. According to a 1993 survey, lawyers at some federal agencies and departments typically *work* an average of 2,038 hours a year. That breaks down to 8 hours per day, with a 1 week vacation per year. And that's about five 40-hour workweeks less than associates in New York, who *bill* 2,000 hours. On top of that, public sector attorneys don't have clients to bill, so they don't have to track billable hours. In spite of the fact that large firms pay so much more than public sector jobs, the freedom from amassing and tracking billables is a big factor in job satisfaction.

On a day-to-day basis, these annualized figures aren't terribly important. Like many large-firm associates, I found that I met my firm's expectations of annual billables simply by completing the work that was assigned to me. Instead, the headache on a daily basis is keeping track of who gets billed for what. The reason for this is that most firms require their associates to keep track of their time in excruciating detail, to ensure that clients are billed correctly. Typically, firms break time into 6-minute chunks (which are tenths of an hour), so they have the flexibility to charge clients for brief tasks, like short phone conversations, as well as for larger projects, like research assignments. It's hard for me to convey just how burdensome this system is! It makes you pay attention to the actual minutes dedicated to each particular matter. By way of example, how many minutes have you spent reading about billable hours? Was it more than 6? Was it more than 12?

Large firms expect you to account, in these tiny increments, for at least 7 hours of work each day, both billable and nonbillable. You have to describe time you spent, in detail, on time sheets that you submit each day. On the next page is a sample daily time sheet.

What happens if you fail to bill a sufficient number of daily hours? A partner may notify and/or warn you that, in the firm's view, you should be billing more hours. As a result, associates generally try to beat the daily minimum requirements, by working longer hours and minimizing nonbillable time.

If you have a dim view of the hourly system, after even this brief introduction to it, you're not alone. It's a constant source of irritation to lawyers, and brings a host of problems to practicing law. Chief Justice William Rehnquist, of the United States Supreme Court, has observed that the pressure on large firm lawyers to bill more than 2,000 hours per year may make them curtail their productive expenditure of energy outside of work, spend excessive time researching issues, and specialize in narrow fields of law—all of which may contribute to job dissatisfaction.

The hourly system creates other problems, as well. For one thing, it promotes inefficiency by eliminating the incentive for law firms to be efficient. Simply put, if a law firm bills more hours, it increases its revenues. If it saves

Daily Time Sheet

Name: John Doe   *Date:* May 5

Client and Matter Number	*Description of Work*	*Time*
Resources Unlimited, Inc. 18785-1002	Telephone call with R. Jones and M. Smith; review documents in connection with upcoming deposition; telephone conference with B. Howell regarding use of company assets.	2.8
Computer Technologies, Ltd. 19978-1001	Meet with A. Barney and S. Deluca regarding projected earnings and quarterly corporate disclosures; telephone conference with P. Castle regarding same	2.4
GHT Enterprises, Inc. 19467-1000	Research New York law regarding a corporate director's duty to exercise care.	1.8
General Systems Corporation 19888-1004	Telephone conference with D. Kane regarding feedback on draft brief.	1.4
First Bank of New York 19976-1001	Meet with G. Lowry, J. Kopple, B. Dirkson, F. Smith, and R. Fraska regarding contractual language to be adopted.	3.1
Office Administration 99999-1000	Organize files	.3

time, it loses revenue. If your firm pressures you to complete assignments quickly, the incentive will be to keep clients happy and meet deadlines—since encouraging you to be more efficient would run contrary to its economic interests.

By the same token, large firm associates have no economic incentive to complete assignments quickly. Paid on salary and paid an annual bonus principally on the basis of billable hours, associates are motivated to complete many billable hours—not assignments. As I found, if you complete your work more efficiently, your reward is more billable work, not more leisure time. However, once you're comfortable with the facts of a case, you simply lack the incentive to resolve the case, since you'll just have to start the arduous task of learning a *new* case. As you might imagine, in response to the pressure to bill a sufficient number of billable hours, some attorneys engage in the unethical and fraudulent practice of "padding" their time sheets—that is, recording more time than they actually spend on particular matters. They abandon ethical conduct and risk disbarment and criminal penalties, all in an effort to keep pace with their peers and secure bonuses and raises.

The hourly system has other, less obvious drawbacks, as well. For one thing, it pits the economic interests of partners against associates. Partners have an equity interest in the law firm; that is, they earn revenue based on the revenues of the firm, and so will want associates to work the maximum possible billable hours. Associates, on the other hand, as salaried employees, have an economic interest in working as *few* hours as possible. For every additional hour worked, an associate's hourly pay goes *down*.

To illustrate this, let's say you're a first year associate at a large firm, earning $83,000. Your firm charges $150 per hour for your services. If you work 2000 billable hours per year, your pretax hourly wage is $41.50, and the pretax revenue you produce for your firm is $300,000. At 2,500 billable hours, your hourly wage drops to $33.20 an hour, while the revenue you bring to the firm increases to $375,000. At 3000 billable hours, your hourly wage drops to $27.67, but you bring in $450,000. Clearly, it's in your firm's best interest to squeeze as many billable hours as possible out of you, because it has to pay you your $83,000 salary and benefits no matter *how* many billable hours you work.

Another problem with the hourly system is that it doesn't ensure a relationship between quality and fees. Instinctively, you'd expect a client to pay more for better work. But when fees are determined solely on the basis of time expended, the focus on quality is lost. A firm simply shouldn't be paid more than other firms to solve the same legal problem just because it took longer to solve a problem. And similarly, a firm shouldn't be punished because it solved the problem more quickly. The same logic applies internally to firms, as well. Since associates are rewarded primarily on the basis of the number of hours they bill, *inefficient* associates may receive higher bonuses than *efficient* associates! As a result, the hourly system creates rewards that defy common sense.

These flaws with the hourly system have led clients, in recent years, to more and more often demand to be billed on a fixed fee basis. With a fixed fee system, law firms and clients negotiate a fixed fee at the start of a case or a deal, based on estimates of the amount of work required. You can immediately see the benefits of such a system. Since the firm *loses* money the more time it takes on a project, it will have the incentive to work quickly and efficiently. Working for a fixed fee also curbs the incidence of "churning," the unethical practice of performing unnecessary legal work in order to bill clients for extra hours. Of course, attorneys who work for fixed fees may not work *less* than colleagues who bill by the hour—but their focus turns to completing projects rather than billing hours.

Law firms use a variety of other methods to increase their profits, some of which are controversial. One common revenue generator is to charge premiums on administrative expenses which arguably should be passed along to clients without a markup. For instance, many large firms tack a premium of 20% or more on the cost of phone calls they make for clients. Similarly, large firms often charge their clients more than 20¢ for photocopies that cost the firms just a few cents. And they frequently charge a dollar or two to send a single fax page, even though their cost is a small fraction of that. Of course, firms charge these premiums in an effort to earn profits any way possible. And while you can argue whether or not these charges are legitimate, they are paltry in comparison to the most effective way a firm can boost its profits—by increasing the number of billable hours it charges its clients.

December 19

Three months at the firm, and I did my first all-nighter last night. It wasn't much fun.

The documents in the Caltrex case have to be in the U.S. Attorney's office in Miami by 10:00 a.m. Monday morning. Since there's no overnight Sunday delivery, we had to ship the 36 boxes of documents—about 50,000 documents—by this afternoon at the latest. Unfortunately, as of yesterday evening, Peter and I were still reviewing the countless documents for privilege. We didn't even start boxing them up for shipment until about 8:00 p.m. It was all pretty mind-numbing.

The pathetic part is that I actually thought we might finish on Friday by about 10:00 or 11:00 p.m. But as we started organizing and boxing the documents, time began to pass unbelievably fast. Everything took longer than expected because we were making sure there were no mistakes. The last thing we wanted to do in a criminal investigation was screw up the document production.

We finished at about 5:00 a.m. this morning. Needless to say, it wasn't a great way to spend our Friday night. I woke up groggy at about 11:00 a.m. and was in the office an hour later just to make sure that the documents had been picked up and that there were no loose ends. I gave Peter a call to let him know that everything was OK and then came home to take a nap.

Every person who joins a large firm as an associate has heard about the long hours they'll have to put in. But there's a kind of self-deceptive game that some large-firm recruits play: "Well, even though everybody else has to work weekends, *I* won't have to. I'll get everything done during the week so I won't *have* to show up on weekends."

If you believe this, you're kidding yourself. Long hours and big firms go hand-in-hand. You'll work harder and longer than you ever have before. And like every new associate at every large law firm in America, you can routinely expect to put in 60 to 100-hour workweeks. You won't do that *every* week—but you'll do it often enough to make you feel like you live to work.

Apart from the sheer fatigue of working gruesome hours, you'll find a zero-sum gain relationship between your work and your social life. The extra time you spend working will come at the direct expense of your leisure activities and social life. Why, you may be asking yourself, are so many people willing to make sacrifices like this? There are several reasons. Most obviously, if your firm assigns you large amounts of work—and it will—you just won't be able to fit it all into a normal, 9-to-5 day. We've already discussed the idea that law firms prosper as they squeeze more billable hours from their associates—and so they do just that.

Another factor contributing to a new associate's willingness to work long hours is that it's the price you pay to get interesting work with significant responsibility. Large firms just won't entrust you with important matters before you've had a lot of quality experiences and exhibited a sufficient level of dedication. Frankly, to large firms the word "dedication" has just one, hidden meaning: "tremendous personal sacrifices." Cruel as it seems, as a new associate you have to decide at some point what your priorities are: your career, or your personal and family life. If you choose your life outside of work, you'll find yourself rejecting additional work, and your reluctance to accept it will brand you as "lacking dedication"—and your career will suffer accordingly.

Clients also contribute directly to the massive hours new associates have to work, by making demands for legal services that require immediate attention. You may have a client, for instance, who needs you to move for a temporary restraining order ("TRO") on its behalf. Or a client may ask you to substantially revise a brief shortly before a court deadline. With emergencies like these, you have to work hard, and you've got to work right now—and that can have a devastating effect on your personal and family life. You may be called upon at a moment's notice to cancel evening or weekend social plans you might have made, vacations you've long anticipated, and even holiday celebrations. Life at a large firm means learning to accept these incidents as occupational risks.

Of course, the pressure to work long hours is not *all* external. The personality that leads people to become attorneys—being enterprising, industrious, and goal-oriented, seeking out opportunities, willingly expressing their opinions, and participating in activities around them —frequently creates a lot of self-generated pressure. If you're reading this book because you're thinking about a large-firm career, you may see yourself in that description. If so, when you get to a large firm as a new associate, you'll find that no matter how heavy your caseload already is, you'll probably want to get involved in activities that further reduce your leisure time—like participating on recruiting committees at the firm, working on *pro bono* cases to help the needy, and taking part in bar association activities. Like other attorneys, you'll probably even put your work and work-related social obligations ahead of your desire to take vacations—which is why many attorneys don't take the vacation time they're given.

The culture at large law firms also pressures new associates to work long hours. As a new associate at a large firm, you'll work at least 11 hours a day. Although your day may typically not start until 9:30, or even later, there's no 5 o'clock whistle at the end of the day. Because large firm attorneys are paid so well, they are expected to work until the job is done, or at least until they're confident they can meet their deadlines. In practice, this means that most large firm attorneys work late—until 9 or 10 at night, and beyond—at least once or twice a week. If they're working on a big project or a case coming to a climax, that pace might go on for several weeks or months. It's not surprising that with hours like these, two-thirds of lawyers say that they frequently feel worn out by the end of the day.

As a new associate, office politics will play a heavy role in your decision to stay late. Most first year associates feel uncomfortable regularly being among the first to leave the office—you're especially uncomfortable taking off if your supervising attorney is still working. Some supervising attorneys even *require* you to stay until they themselves leave. On top of that, you frequently find eager first year associates determined to show their dedication by regularly being the first one in and the last one to leave. With colleagues like this, as a new associate you're wise to show, at least occasionally, comparable dedication to ensure that you're perceived as a hard worker—a trait highly prized by senior attorneys.

Adjusting to long working hours is a particular challenge if you've never had a full-time career before, and went straight from college to law school, as I did. It's a tremendous leap from the academic lifestyle—replete with physical activity, naps, stimulating intellectual debates, and a vigorous social calendar—to the rigors of working for a large firm. Even new associates who *did* work full-time before law school find the transition difficult, because the long hours and pressures of large-firm practice are unique. It's difficult to learn the necessary survival skills in any other context. On top of that, people who've held other professional positions have the added burden of adjusting to being the "low man on the totem pole" in a second career.

Long hours for lawyers today are more stressful than for lawyers in years gone by, because an hour's work today is far more stressful than it was for lawyers even 30 years ago. As the American Bar Association's Young Lawyers Division noted in 1990, "The pressures and demands of law firms and clients, the element of speed created by the advent of fax machines and computers, and the increasing lack of courtesy between lawyers—to name just a few of the factors that create strain for lawyers—have together changed the quality of the hours worked so that 200 hours in today's practice is far more stressful than 200 hours in the 1960s." Pile the pressurized contents of work hours on top of the sheer volume of hours worked, and you've got a recipe for misery.

A problem separate and distinct from the number of hours you work as a new associate is the unpredictable nature of those hours—a factor that adds even more pressure to an already tense job environment.

December 23

I'm still in shock as I write this entry. I can't believe I'm getting dogged like this 2 days before Christmas.

At about 4:30 p.m. today, I got a call from Allen, a partner for whom I've never worked. I knew it was going to be bad when he started with an apology. I was right. He said that he needed me "to research some case law and put together some ideas over the weekend" for Connor Industries. We apparently have to file a response brief with the First Circuit by next Wednesday, and Karen, the attorney who normally works for Connor, is out of the country for the holidays.

I could hardly believe my ears as Allen explained the assignment. Was I crazy, or did he want me to draft an appellate brief in a case that I had never worked on before? Over Christmas weekend? Was this guy for real? Was this some kind of test? What about all the work I still have to do for the Caltrex case?

Despite my primal desire to tell Allen to go to hell, I sucked it up.

I told him that I had plans to visit my family for Christmas but that I'll take the relevant cases with me and do an initial draft. I wondered to myself how I was even going to get the cases before I left, let alone draft the damn brief.

I got off the phone and regrouped. I knew I had to start finding cases immediately. I started researching and made a list of all the potentially relevant cases. Then I rounded up three paralegals and had them start finding and copying the cases.

Fortunately, most of the cases had been copied by the time I left work. Tomorrow is Christmas Eve, and the office is going to be open only half the day. I'll get whatever else I need in the morning and then get the hell out of there. I'm not going to let this brief ruin my Christmas.

It's difficult enough to work long hours. But that problem is exacerbated by the fact that at a large firm, those hours aren't just long, they're *unpredictable*. In fact, associates who are dissatisfied with large firm practice are twice as likely to want to leave because of the unpredictability of their hours, as opposed to their length. And, like working long hours, there's no way to get around this unpredictability if you're going to work for a large firm.

What creates this unpredictability? There are a few culprits. One significant one, at least in the minds of some associates, is that assignments are distributed unevenly and unfairly. It may be that your firm has a poorly functioning work-delegation system, and that's what leads to canceled social plans and hurt feelings. But there are other reasons for unpredictable hours that are *outside* of a large firm's control. Unexpected work often comes up when clients have an emergency—real or perceived—that requires immediate legal assistance or counseling. This will inevitably require at least a little bit of research, and, as a junior associate, you'll be the one to bear the brunt of that research. So if one of your clients needs a quick response from you or your supervising attorney late in the day, you'll have a long night. Worse yet, if they need it on a Friday afternoon, you'll probably wind up canceling any significant weekend plans you have.

As you might imagine, the newer you are, the more of a problem unpredictable hours are. As a first year associate, you're analogous to a young soldier positioned at the front of battle troops so that the generals are protected and positioned to see the "big picture" of an ensuing battle. Like the soldier, you'll be at the proverbial "front line," and *your* personal time will often be sacrificed to protect that of partners and senior associates.

Often, you'll receive no advance warning of assignments. Typically, a more senior attorney wanting to delegate work to you will call you—at work or at home—and ask whether you have time to do an assignment. If you want to stay in good standing at the firm, it's a good idea to respond "yes," with enthusiasm. The nature of the work —and your huge paycheck—means that you're expected to accept and complete work willingly, unless you already have a pressing deadline or you're so burdened with other work that you legitimately can't spread yourself any thinner by accepting another assignment.

Another element that contributes to the state of uncertainty that you live in as a junior associate is that you never know the timing, complexity, or size of your next assignment. You get additional assignments when they're least expected—and when you're least able to manage them.

Even though this is a problem common to *all* lawyers in any firm, no matter how senior they are, it's a bigger problem for new associates. That's because, as a junior attorney, the odds are against you—there are simply more lawyers who can assign work to you. As a first year associate, you are, at least theoretically, at the mercy of every lawyer in your firm (other than the *other* first year associates). Your lack of control is heightened by the fact that your inexperience leaves you needing supervision. That impacts your autonomy, because you must, to some extent, bend to the schedule of the attorney supervising you. Also, as a junior attorney, you're "out of the loop" on developments in any particular case the firm is handling, because you're not supervising the progress of the case. That means you lack the information necessary to anticipate your workload and plan your personal life.

This all adds up to a feeling as a new associate that you are always "on call," regardless of how hard you try to plan your work. I found—as most junior attorneys do— that I wound up making tentative social plans, and always qualified my intent to attend *any* social function by mentioning that my work might interfere. By the same token, as a new associate you learn quickly to deal with your disappointment when you can't attend a long-cherished social event. To avoid this, there are attorneys who actually take off the preceding day to reduce the risk of being "found" by a client or another attorney and having to work through an important event.

One of my friend Rob's experiences at the firm reflects how intrusive being "on call" can become. Rob had plans to spend the weekend visiting his mother in southern New Jersey, and was hiding out hoping not to get nailed by a senior attorney looking for someone to work over the weekend. As it happened, the office was quiet that afternoon, and he was able to escape by about 6 p.m. without incident, and without telling anyone where he could be reached. Ordinarily, a Friday afternoon escape would not necessarily mean a free weekend, but on this occasion, Rob slipped into the elevator unnoticed and basked in the joy of knowing that he was completely free for the next 36 hours.

After a great weekend with his mother, Rob was driving back from New Jersey and decided to retrieve his messages using his car phone. Sure enough, there were two messages from Brad, who said he needed to speak with Rob as soon as he got in. The fact that Brad had called twice made Rob nervous. One call would have meant that Brad was looking for any available grunt associate to do some weekend work; two calls meant that Brad was looking for a specific grunt named Rob.

As soon as he got home, about 9 o'clock, Rob called Brad at home. Brad was out, and his children's nanny answered the phone. She told Rob that Brad was out, and Rob left a message that he'd be home, hoping against hope that Brad would get home too late to call. No such luck; an hour later, the phone rang. Rob answered, "Hello?"

Brad jumped right into the conversation without bothering to say hello. "Well, where the f**k have *you* been?" Brad asked, half-jokingly, but his clear message was: what sort of social life could you possibly have, and why weren't you home when I needed you?

On the one hand, Rob was stunned at Brad's rudeness. On the other, he was excited, because he knew he had a great answer, "I was visiting my mom."

It was one of the best answers he could have given. Here was a young guy who, when he finally got a free weekend, spent it visiting his mother.

Rob's response set Brad back, and was followed by a 3- or 4-second pause. Brad eventually just mumbled the cliché, "Oh, that's nice," before getting down to business with his customary lead-in: "Listen, here's what I need you to do. . . ."

Rob was lucky that he escaped that weekend, and lucky that he had such a great excuse when Brad called him on it. But if you become a large firm associate, there's no telling when *you* might have to cancel a much anticipated vacation because of an emergency at work. If you've ever planned a vacation, you know how difficult it is to make *tentative* plans, because you normally have to reserve airline tickets and hotels well in advance. As a large-firm associate, you're informed, overtly or subtly, that you might need to cancel your vacation if you can't be spared. Of course, the firm will reimburse you for any expenses you've already incurred, but that is faint consolation to you, your family, and/or significant others. Often there *is* a warm body at a large firm who can take your place, but you don't have to cancel many vacations to become dispirited about your work.

April 5

I had my review today.

This morning, my telephone rang with an internal ring. The usual questions ran through my head. Would I get more work if I picked it up? Should I let it bounce to Jill? I didn't feel like talking to anyone, but I answered it anyway.

"Bill," I heard, "this is Dan." Dan is the partner in charge of recruiting and he reviews a number of associates each fall. He speaks very differently depending on his mood and the amount of stress he happens to be feeling at the moment. I could tell he was in a good mood by the way he extended the pronunciation of my name,

letting his voice get higher as he said the last portion of it and then letting his voice drop as he identified himself.

Dan and I chatted a few moments before he informed me that it was time for my review. He was calling to find out when we could get together for it. My schedule was pretty open, and we settled on 4:30 p.m.

To be sure, I was a little nervous. I certainly wasn't afraid of losing my job—I knew I hadn't made any grievous mistakes and that I had played the office politics game fairly well. But I had questions for which I had no answers. Was I any good at the practice of law? Did I do a less than adequate job on any of my assignments? How did I compare with other first year associates? Was I billing enough hours? It was the fear of the unknown that bothered me.

I stopped by Dan's office at 4:30 p.m. and found him typing on his computer. He invited me in and got right down to business. He had apparently already reviewed my file because he began by giving me an overview of my performance. He then pulled out my file and scanned each written evaluation, quoting and paraphrasing parts of each. I was relieved to learn that everyone I've worked for gave me favorable evaluations. I assume Dan would have told me if I had pissed anybody off.

When he finished reading the evaluations, Dan asked me—with pen in hand—whether I had any comments or complaints. I had plenty of complaints, but as someone who's been at the firm for less than a year, I wasn't about to tell them to him so that he could record them in my permanent personnel file.

Besides, I can't believe that my comments would have even the slightest impact on working conditions. The partnership and office management have spent years devising policies and shaping *working conditions so as to maximize the firm's profitability. I just can't believe that my opinions as a first year associate—a fungible asset that, according to statistics, will burn out after a few years and move on—will impact decision-making within the firm.*

Exercising great restraint, I told Dan that I had enjoyed working at the firm and that my job was everything that I had hoped it would be. Familiar with the standard associate answer, he smiled knowingly, and told me to keep up the good work.

Overall, it went pretty well.

Most large law firms believe that associate reviews are critical to their associates' development. At least in theory, associate reviews give associates constructive criticism and feedback, and give them a chance to articulate concerns about their work environments, assignments, and careers. As every junior associate knows, however, you'd have to be *crazy* to use your review as a forum for criticizing the firm, no matter *how* much you hate your job.

As a new associate, at most large firms you can expect to have your job performance reviewed twice a year during your first year, and once a year thereafter (although associates who are perceived as underperformers tend to go on being reviewed twice a year). What happens is that all of the attorneys who supervise you more than a minimal number of hours (for instance, 10 hours) since you started working for the firm, or since your last review, will provide a written evaluation of your performance.

Predictably, every year you spend with the firm makes it more and more difficult to get favorable reviews, because more is expected from you as you progress from researching discrete issues to managing cases and maintaining good relations with clients. As a senior associate who might be considered for partnership in a year or two, you'd expect to be more closely scrutinized than a wet-behind-the-ears new associate.

However, that doesn't mean that reviews as a new associate aren't stressful. They are. For one thing, they don't provide the outlet you'd expect for expressing concerns about your work environment, your assignments, or your career. I've talked with junior associates who made the mistake of taking their reviewing partner into their confidence to express their concerns about their job, only to be branded negatively as a result. It's important to bear in mind that *any* comments you make, positive or negative, are noted in your permanent personnel file. On top of that, it's unlikely that complaining about the long hours or the boring assignments would result in any positive changes. So, as a first year associate, if your working conditions won't change even if you complain about them, you'll probably find—as most junior associates do—that it's simply more politically prudent to tell your reviewing partner that you're content with your job, no matter how you really feel about it.

Associate reviews are also flawed in that they don't provide the level of feedback that most junior associates want. Most people who become first year associates at large firms are fresh out of law school where they received regular feedback in the form of grades. When you start to work at a large firm, you'll find a strong urge for the same kind of feedback; in fact, you'd ideally like a "grade" from your supervising attorney after each assignment. *Without* that kind of feedback, you inevitably start to wonder about whether your work is adequate. On top of that, since your firm will push you and your colleagues to rack up billable hours, you'll find yourself searching for reasons to believe that your firm cares about your professional development, and not just about money.

Regardless of those concerns, most large firms simply do not provide feedback between annual or semiannual reviews. Instead, they expect your work-product to meet very high standards. Your ability to meet or exceed those standards is considered a job requirement as opposed to a talent worthy of recognition. Although most law firms promise law students during interviews that they provide substantial feedback, virtually no firm lives up to that promise.

Instead, the uncertainty you feel as a first year associate will remind you of how you felt during your first semester in college or law school. That is, no matter how well you performed in the past, you'll have doubts about how well you're doing *now,* in this new environment. Almost all first year associates ask themselves, "Am I any good at practicing law?" If you can't answer this question with a truthful and confident "yes," you'll face your review with considerable anxiety.

April 13

I got back from lunch today and saw the voice mail light on my phone blinking. With my overcoat still on, I picked up the phone and retrieved the message, hoping it would be a message from one of my friends rather than a new assignment. Consistent with my usual luck, it was Greg, a partner for whom I've never worked. He wanted me to stop by his office to talk about my availability for an article he wants written.

When I got to Greg's office, we caught up a bit before getting down to business. We don't talk very often because we're on different floors and we do different work—I'm a litigator and he does mostly corporate and banking work. That's why I wasn't worried about getting stuck on his project. I knew Brad, a more senior litigation partner and a bigger rainmaker, wouldn't let me take on any additional work, let alone corporate work.

Greg eventually steered the conversation toward his proposed article by noting that we hadn't worked together yet and that it would be nice if we could. Of course, I agreed. He explained that he needed help over the next 3 months preparing an article on banking regulations for submission to a banking industry regulatory organization. I feigned interest as I listened and thought that I'd get screwed unless I could duck the assignment—I'd get caught between two partners doing work I didn't want to do. He finished his overview and asked me whether I'd be interested in helping out.

That was my cue. I was ready. I delivered my speech like I had been practicing it in my head. I told Greg that I thought the article sounded interesting and that I'd be glad to help out to the extent I could; that my only concern was that Brad already had me working full-time and weekends on the Infomax case; and that I wouldn't mind unloading some of the Infomax work as long as Brad says it's OK.

Greg suddenly realized he was going to have to ask Brad for permission to use me. There was an awkward pause as Greg nodded, contemplating whether he should take on Brad in a battle of office politics. He knew he'd probably lose; Brad needs as many warm bodies as he can get for the Infomax case, and would never release me to do nonbillable, corporate work. Thankfully, Greg came through with the expected response. He said that while it was a shame, he didn't think I'd have enough time for the article. He *explained that he needed someone who could spend the better part of the next few months working on it, and that I probably wouldn't be able to commit enough time to it. I agreed and reiterated that I'd be glad to help out any way I could. He'll probably never mention the article to me again.*

Mission accomplished.

Large firms can pay big salaries because they generate big fees. One way they get clients to part with those large fees is to convince clients that they have a special expertise not shared by other firms. And one means of accomplishing that is to show clients lists of publications by their attorneys, the theory being that if a firm's lawyers generate articles about a topic, they must be experts on it.

These publications are particularly useful to large firms when they're taking part in "beauty contests." A beauty contest comes about when a potential client, usually a corporation, needs legal help on a case, and it requests contending law firms to submit proposals. These proposals typically summarize the relevant law, describe the legal services the matter will likely require, and propose an approach to resolve the problem, as well as a fee estimate and the résumés of the lawyers who'd likely work on the case. If a firm has lawyers who have published articles on the issue facing the client, this clearly gives them a leg up in the beauty contest—and that's where the push to publish comes from.

You've probably already guessed that partners who can demand hundreds of dollars an hour for their services are hardly going to pore over books in the law firm's library for hours on end, generating articles—regardless of how well those articles reflect on the firm. Instead, that task is delegated to junior associates, and as a first year associate you're very likely to be pressed into service to draft at least a portion of an article for a partner.

I should clarify what I'm talking about when I talk about "articles," because you may be thinking of the articles that you read in magazines and you may say to yourself, "Well, writing articles wouldn't be so bad." The problem is that I'm not talking about the kind of thing that you typically read. Instead, I'm talking about articles that appear in scholarly legal publications. If you're in law school, you're very familiar with at least at one scholarly publication, your school's "law review." Every law school in the country has a law review. These law reviews publish articles that are typically between 10 and 50 pages long. Each article analyzes a discrete legal issue, and expresses an opinion on how that issue should be addressed. In addition, there are scholarly publications for just about every specialty and subspecialty you can imagine.

These articles *can*, and sometimes are, used as a secondary authority for legal researchers, lawyers, and courts. That is, they are used to support positions, arguments, and judicial decisions, even though they aren't binding authority. So you might find articles that look at trends in the judiciary or legal profession, or predict the impact of an important judicial decision, or examine how a particular legal doctrine should be applied to an emerging body of law. I had a friend, for instance, who wrote a law review article about whether people could be held liable for infecting other people with sexually transmitted diseases, like AIDS or herpes.

Of course, large firms aren't likely to have you write articles on topics like that, because they're interested in publishing articles that will improve their credentials and attract clients, and so the topics they choose are typically far from controversial. As a junior attorney, you don't have to worry about generating article ideas yourself; your supervising attorney gives you the topic when you're asked to write the article.

With such an assignment in hand, you do the research and draft the article, and then your supervising attorney reviews and edits it, and then submits it to the various law reviews for publication. The supervising attorney gets credit as an author or coauthor because they supervised your work.

As a junior associate, your willingness to write articles depends on a number of considerations: your workload, the subject matter of the article, and your fondness for writing are obvious concerns. But there are others that aren't so obvious. For instance, a significant benefit of article writing is that it increases your marketability in the legal community. Just as an article enhances your firm's expertise in a certain area, if your name appears on the article as author or coauthor, your own reputation improves at the same time. This is an important point to remember, because it's very easy as a junior associate to overlook the importance of demanding coauthor credit and let the supervising attorney get all the credit for writing an article that you, in fact, wrote largely by yourself. If you've got a string of publications when you're looking for subsequent jobs elsewhere, you've got tangible proof of your expertise. On top of that, your name on your publications can help give you an identity of your own in the legal community, on top of just being associated with your firm. If you've got any dreams of becoming a law professor after you practice for a few years—as many people do—then you'll find that publications are crucial to your ultimate success.

Many associates find that articles provide a valuable creative outlet. Contrary to popular belief, working at a large firm actually provides very little opportunity to be creative. Writing articles that explore novel legal issues helps alleviate some of the boredom that comes about from typical junior-associate level assignments, like document reviews.

On top of that, writing articles involves very little stress, because articles don't involve the strict deadlines that accompany most assignments. You find that you just don't have to "burn the midnight oil" for an article, which makes them a perfect back-burner project.

So why don't *all* junior associates relish writing articles? There are a number of good reasons. My colleague, Glenn, told me that he didn't want to write articles because he was sick of theory; he wanted "real" legal work—that is, work directed toward solving a client's legal problems.

Other junior associates avoid writing articles because it's nonbillable work. I've stressed the importance of piling up billable hours as a new attorney. Writing articles, because it can't be billed to any client, doesn't count as billable time, and so even people who *like* writing articles try not to do too much of it. While it's true that any work you do, billable or nonbillable, gets evaluated when your performance at the firm is reviewed, your firm naturally won't value the time you dedicate to articles as highly as billable work, because nonbillable work doesn't make the lease payments on the luxury car, does it? Furthermore, nonbillable work doesn't help you rack up the minimum annual billables your firm will expect from you, expressly or impliedly. If this sounds negative, remember that law firms are businesses. As a result, your ability to improve your firm's bottom line will, throughout your career, improve your stature within the firm. Writing articles doesn't do that, at least not directly—and that's why it's a good idea not to devote *too* much time to them, even if writing is something you enjoy.

May 24

The summer associates started today. I can't believe the summer is here already. Time is flying by.

We kicked off the program with a typical welcome breakfast for all the summer associates. Overall, it seems like we've got a good group of people, although a few seem like they need to get out more. Fortunately, one or two seem athletic enough to help carry our softball team. I spent most of my time talking with Steve, a Harvard Law School student who just completed his second year. I'm Steve's "mentor" for the summer, so I figured we should get to know each other.

At about 12:30 p.m., Rob and I took Steve and Lynn, another summer associate, to lunch at a swank French restaurant. Neither Rob nor I had any pressing work and we both wanted to milk the firm's summer associate budget for a long, leisurely lunch. Besides, Christine told us we could spend a little more than usual because it was the summer associates' first day.

Over a 2-hour lunch (during which we stuffed ourselves), Rob and I got to know Steve and Lynn pretty well. They seem like they're genuine, sincere and fun. In fact, I'm looking forward to playing softball and joining in on some of the other summer associate events. But I'm torn between being myself around them and maintaining the image of a "model" associate. Frank Boyle's sudden termination last summer is testimony to the importance of "toeing the firm line."

Everyone knows that one of the reasons he was fired was for bad-mouthing the firm to the summer associates.

They might have fooled me, but I think Steve and Lynn both want to join big firms when they graduate. They seem so naive—it's downright amusing to see how little they know about working in a law firm. It's hard to believe I was just like them as a law student. Reality is going to slap them silly.

Every large law firm vies for the services of the same, tiny group of top law students. Firms have expensive, elaborate recruiting programs to help ensure that they get the best of the best. And the crown jewel of those recruiting programs is the summer associate program. Each fall, large firms invite a select number of law school students to work full-time during the following summer. The students work—although "work" may be too strong a word for it—for 2 or 3 months, at the staggering sum of more than $1,500 per week. Then the students return to school, hoping that they've performed well enough to receive an offer of permanent employment (if they're going to graduate next year) or an invitation to return the following summer (if they're still in school).

The ostensible reason that large firms run summer associate programs is to find out who they want as permanent associates. The idea is that by having an opportunity to view students for a summer, they can evaluate their work quality, motivation, work ethic, potential for success, and whether the student's personality will fit the firm mold.

Large firms certainly have a strong economic incentive for using their summer associate programs to figure out who ought to receive permanent offers after law school.

That's because large firms spend obscene amounts of money on first year associates. The researcher Eric Gebaide estimates that between expenses for office space, professional and health insurance, moving expenses, bar expenses, secretarial salary, and benefits packages, a law firm spends more than *half a million dollars* on each first year associate. As you might imagine, that economic risk makes most firms think very carefully about extending permanent offers to students who *didn't* participate in the firm's summer associate program.

That would lead you to think that a summer associate program would be a great conduit to permanent employment. Ironically, that's not the case. Gebaide found that less than half of the people who join large firms as permanent associates were part of that firm's summer associate program as students. And as you move through the ranks, the numbers decrease; less than a third of senior associates were summer associates at their firm.

That leads to the conclusion that summer associate programs must serve another function. Gebaide theorizes that the programs produce a sought after "ambassadorial" effect. He thinks that the "silent purpose" of summer associate programs is to have the summer associates act as "ambassadors" for the firm when they go back to school in the fall. In fact, during his research he found that summer associates who had a good experience at a firm proved to be great walking advertisements for the firm, enhancing that firm's ability to lure top students. To the extent that Gebaide is right, law students become unwitting pawns in the recruiting game.

Regardless of the function, large firms spend huge amounts of money on their summer associate programs—typically between $80,000 and $100,000. A budget like that gives a large firm several advantages over smaller firms with less money to spend on summer associates.

For one thing, a well-funded summer program can include many law students. That gives the firm more opportunities to recruit what they perceive as top legal talent, including students who otherwise might not have considered working for a large firm. From a law student's perspective, a large summer associate program creates more job opportunities. In an era when legal jobs of *any* kind are increasingly rare, a summer job that pays as well as a large-firm summer clerkship—in the neighborhood of $12,000 for a summer—is obviously welcome.

A large summer program budget also gives large firms the chance to shower summer associates with lavish surroundings and expensive social activities. Large firms routinely take their summer associates to fine restaurants, sometimes three or four times a week. Standard social activities, all courtesy of the firm, include boat trips, movie premieres, the theater, sports tickets (typically in the firm's luxury box), and softball leagues. All too often, these well-funded programs have a substantial influence on impoverished law students who are enticed by the apparent abundance of money. The pay and benefits can act as a sort of anesthetic, numbing the student to looking at the kind of work (s)he'll have to perform if (s)he becomes a permanent associate at the firm.

The economic benefits of summer associate programs don't all flow from the large firm to the summer associates. The firms benefit financially, as well. During their stint at the firm, summer associates typically "rotate" through the firm's various departments, the idea being to give the student exposure to different kinds of practice, and to meet (and, ideally, impress) as many of the firm's attorneys as possible. As they move through the departments, the summer associates are given assignments, and they keep track of the billable time on those projects. In turn, the firm will bill its clients for the work its summer associates perform. Of course, the billing rate for a summer associate is less than for a permanent associate, but it's still not cheap—a billing rate for a summer clerk may run well over a hundred dollars an hour. Remember, this is a bill for someone who may be a top student, but has no practical experience at all! Nonetheless, billing a summer associate's time to clients does give the firm a means of earning back the substantial sum it spends on its summer program.

Of course, from a student's perspective, a large firm's summer associate program should offer a bird's-eye view of what it's like to practice law at the firm. Laughably few summer associates actually gain that insight, however. Over the course of the summer, they'll typically attend fun and expensive events, receive interesting work, face few (if any) pressing deadlines, and typically put in an 8-hour day. By the time they return to school, they've had an experience that is inaccurate at best—and calculatedly misleading at worst. My own ability to evaluate my firm during my summer clerkship there was hampered by the fact that I spent 3 weeks working on a case in Denver. While that gave me some insight into business travel— which was still exciting to me at the time!—it did impair my ability to absorb tidbits about life at the firm which might have proven very useful to me.

Even if summer associates learn about the work the firm does, they nonetheless avoid the stress that keeps a choke hold on permanent associates. After all, summer associates know that they'll be leaving at the end of the summer, and that finite employment provides a wonderful psychological security blanket. Even if the firm doesn't make them a permanent offer to come back and work after they graduate, no matter how badly they perform or how bad an impression they make on the attorneys at the firm, they're never at risk of losing their summer associate position.

June 17

Mike and I caught an early flight to Chicago today to meet with Harry Gordon, one of Infomax's Board members, and his lawyers.

As part of our work for Infomax, we've been interviewing certain of its present and former Board members to find out what they knew and thought about a proposed merger before they voted on it. We've been traveling all over the country (Orlando, Sacramento, Tennessee) to meet personally with the Board members and their attorneys. We've been meeting with the Board members in person because their conduct and reactions—verbal and physical—often determine the questions we ask, as well as the tone in which we ask them.

We arrived at the airport with minutes to spare, just as the airline was about to give away our first-class seats. We were the last passengers to board and we hurriedly took our seats. The flight lasted about an hour and a half, and touched down in Chicago at 10:30.

Our meeting was scheduled for 11:30 in the main office of the law firm representing the Board members. We arrived a few minutes early, but Elizabeth, one of Harry's attorneys, invited us to wait in the conference room in which we would be meeting. It was a nice gesture since it gave us access to a phone and enabled us to do some last-minute preparation. She also mentioned that Harry had called her a few moments earlier to say that he was running a little late.

By 11:40 or so, Elizabeth and Tom, a partner also representing Harry, joined us in the conference room. We spoke cordially for a few minutes about Chicago and the White Sox before moving on to the Infomax case. Tom was pressing fairly hard about our work thus far for Infomax's special litigation committee, trying to get a sense of the committee's conclusions thus far. For the most part, Mike and I deflected the questions, although we let them know the committee isn't on a witch hunt.

Within a few minutes, the receptionist called to inform us that Harry had arrived and was waiting in the reception area. Elizabeth left to meet him and escorted him back to the conference room. Harry looked just like I had envisioned him—tall, well-dressed, silver hair, and in his sixties—as if he had been cast for the role. In fact, he looked a lot like most of Infomax's other directors. He apologized for being late and we started the meeting.

As usual, Mike asked virtually all of the questions today, while I took notes. I'd interject every now and then, but Mike was clearly leading the discussion. Even Harry's lawyers didn't need to say much because in this particular litigation, our real adversary at this point is the plaintiff-shareholder, not the Board members. Today's questions were all fairly standard anyway.

At about 12:45, sandwiches and sodas were brought in and we took a short lunch break. Harry dominated most of the conversation, telling us about his background and experiences. He seemed like an interesting guy, but he clearly represented "the old school." The meeting resumed about 20 minutes later and lasted for another *hour or so. All in all, it took about 2 hours, pretty much as long as all the others.*

Mike and I grabbed a cab back to the airport to get the next flight home. While on the plane, I started reviewing my meeting notes and preparing my memorandum discussing the substance of the meeting.

Being a new associate doesn't mean spending *all* of your time with your nose in books and documents, either in the library doing research, or reviewing documents, or drafting memos and articles. You sometimes attend meetings or take part in conference calls with clients, co-counsel, opposing counsel, and other parties. There are a couple of reasons you're asked to take part in these kinds of activities. For instance, they keep you current on a particular case, so that you are better informed when you're asked to research an issue that might arise out of the meeting or call.

Your role in meetings and conference calls can take other forms, as well. For instance, before a meeting or call takes place, your supervising attorney might ask you to prepare "talking points" for them or the client to use during the meeting or call. "Talking points" are usually an outline of points on a particular matter that the attorney or client will want to make. For instance, talking points for a board of directors' meeting usually include an introduction, a review of the legal work already done, a description of any significant obstacles remaining, and a proposed course of action that would help the client overcome these obstacles.

As you might expect, preparing talking points requires you to have a working knowledge of a case. That means that you're normally only asked to prepare talking points if you've been working on the case from its inception, and have a good grasp of the direction the case might take in future.

Preparing talking points can be quite interesting, but another role you might play—taking notes on meetings—isn't. While all of the lawyers at meetings and conference calls will usually take *some* notes, as the most junior associate, you'll be the "official scribe," taking the most detailed and comprehensive set of notes of the discussion. At the very least, you'll be expected to keep your notes of meetings and conference calls in your case files (which are simply all of the papers that pertain to a particular case). Sometimes you'll have to go beyond keeping your notes, and actually prepare what's called a memorandum to the file. That's typically necessary when the meeting involved interviewing a corporate official, or someone at the meeting adopted a particular position or promised to undertake a certain task. Other times, for board of directors' or committee meetings, or like functions, you might have to use your notes to prepare meeting minutes on your client's behalf.

While writing a memorandum to the file or meeting minutes seems like it should be straightforward, it's actually a trap for unwary new associates. That's because new lawyers are rarely sufficiently careful when they write down statements about sensitive subjects, like negligence and liability. As a lawyer you should never create a document that one day might harm your client.

You may find this counterintuitive, especially if you're familiar with the work-product doctrine and the attorney-client privilege, both of which typically protect interview memoranda and similar documents from being disclosed to other parties. But it's dangerous to rely on these protections because they might be waived, intentionally or unintentionally—and that could mean that your notes and memoranda are available to people you never intended to see them. As a result, it's always a good idea to ask yourself when you're preparing a memorandum: "Would my client be harmed if this appeared on the front page of the newspaper?" If your answer is "yes," then you should make any modifications necessary to protect your client.

July 10

Rob and I have been in Boulder, working on a document review for Maxtor Systems for 3 days now.

We've been trying to experience as much of the city as possible, but it's tough because we usually work late and then we're too tired to do anything but go straight to dinner. The food has probably been the most interesting so far. I can now proudly say that I've eaten rattlesnake, buffalo, "Rocky Mountain oysters" (bull testicles), and a whole lot of other food. In fact, it's hard not to overeat. Meals are the only thing we look forward to, and they're free. I've got to start exercising soon—if not my body, at least some self-restraint.

Does the idea of business travel sound exciting to you? Your answer will probably be in inverse proportion to the amount of business travel you've actually had to do. People who *do* have to travel frequently on business generally try to avoid it.

Of course, a lot of other kinds of professionals do a lot of business traveling; lawyers aren't alone in that. But I wanted to mention it here to clue you in to what business travel for lawyers is like, because in some ways it's not like any other kind of business travel.

Why would you travel as a lawyer? You might be participating in a board of directors' meeting or other corporate meeting. Or a settlement conference, or an internal investigation, or a document review, which was how I got to do most of my traveling. Or you might be attending a conference, or seminar, or you may even have a speaking engagement.

Your practice area and seniority determines how frequently you travel. Litigators typically travel more than other specialists, and among litigators, the nature of the project determines how much they'll travel. I traveled frequently because the kinds of assignments I got as a junior associate—document reviews—necessitated my being where the documents were. Other kinds of work, like preparing a compliance manual for a corporate client, wouldn't require travel.

Personality also plays a role in how much any particular lawyer will travel. For example, when your firm sends you to a corporate client's headquarters, you're an ambassador for your firm. That means that firms will typically choose to send extroverted and personable lawyers whenever possible, who will reflect well on the firm.

If you wind up traveling a lot when you practice law, you'll probably develop a love-hate relationship with business travel, like I did. Ironically, many lawyers, while they sit at their desks, wish they could spice up their daily routines with a business trip. But when they're actually on that business trip, at a client's headquarters 2,000 miles away, they yearn for the comforts of their homes, families, and familiar office routines.

The most obvious benefit of business travel is that it gives you a chance to see the country without either consuming vacation time or dipping into your bank account. In fact, your business travel will be an economic windfall. Your client pays your travel expenses—hotel, airfare, meals, everything. And you get to escape your office environment—a particular benefit if it's stressful—and the monotony of your daily office routine.

Business travel also gives you the chance to earn frequent-flyer miles from airlines, and frequent-stay points from hotels. You can use both of these for yourself, personally, when you go on vacation. If you fly frequently for work, or work away from home for an extended period of time, you might accumulate points fairly quickly. Flying frequently also gets you extra perks from the airlines, like free first-class upgrades. If you're particularly ambitious about it, you can use certain credit cards that double your frequent-flyer miles when you use them. You can easily save thousands of dollars on airfare and hotels this way, and to top it off, you don't have to pay income tax on the money you save.

Of course, business travel has its drawbacks, as well. For instance, not *every* trip gives you a chance to get to know a new place. Many business trips are so short and hurried that the only sights you see are the airport and the four walls of a conference room. No matter how pleasant the city, you're there to work. If you want to see more of the city, you'll have to extend your stay, at your own personal expense, to do so.

Especially unpleasant are the overnight trips to a different time zone. What tends to happen is that you return home just as you've adjusted to the time change. And if you travel *very* frequently, you'll have an experience many business travelers learn to dread: the sensation of waking up in a strange bed, looking around the room, and wondering what city you are in.

Longer trips also have their drawbacks. As your time away from home lengthens and the excitement of a new city fades, you'll likely start to resent the travel your job requires. Extended travel can't help but hamper personal relationships, at least in the short-term. By the time your workday is over and you return to your hotel, it will be late and you will be tired. Mustering energy to have a pleasant phone conversation will be difficult. And while telephone calls are important in maintaining a solid, healthy relationship, they are poor substitutes for your actual presence.

Long business trips also throw monkey wrenches into your ability to run even the most mundane aspects of your personal life. Try, for example, doing your banking when you're away on business every day your bank is open. Or try getting an appointment with your favorite hair stylist on a Saturday. Or try doing an entire week's worth of personal events and errands on short weekend trips home, especially when you'll likely have to spend at least part of the weekend at the office working.

On extended stays, even if you get to go home on weekends, you'll find that living in a hotel grows old quickly. Sure, it's nice to have daily maid service. It's one of those things most of us would like to have at home. But hotels can't make up for your home, friends, and family. The more you travel for business, the more you appreciate that.

August 20

Today I was in Boca Raton, Florida, at Allegheny Industries's subsidiary, a manufacturer of construction equipment being investigated by the federal government. I was in the company's managerial offices to speak with Ted Simpson, the company's Chief Financial Officer, but I could hear the drills and welding torches of the nearby assembly line in the background.

Ted has silver-hair and is approaching 50. He's smart, but his intelligence might not be immediately detectable since he's fairly reserved. His most notable characteristic is his biting sarcasm, and he was in rare form today.

When I poked my head into his office, I saw his nose deep in his accounting books. I knocked on his open door and asked him if he had a few minutes.

Ted looked up and grinned. He told me to come in, and, very sarcastically, told me how happy he was to see me. We chit-chatted for a few minutes before I asked for his help in locating some documents and in understanding the mechanics of the company's accounting system.

Ted was very helpful, especially in explaining how the company keeps its books and inventory. He even diagrammed the accounting system on a chalkboard in his office—an act that exceeded his usual level of enthusiasm and cooperation. As I was leaving, I thanked him and, jokingly, assured him that I would bother him again if I needed any additional help.

Reverting to his usual sarcasm, Ted said that he couldn't wait for me to stop by again. But then he paused and grew serious. Shaking his head slightly, he said that while he probably shouldn't joke so much in light of the seriousness of the investigation, he just doesn't like lawyers.

I shrugged it off and told him not to worry—no one does.

You probably don't need to be told that lawyers in the United States are battling a severe image crisis—and that if and when you yourself become a lawyer, you'll battle it on a personal level, too. Many factors contribute to the public's increasingly negative perception of lawyers. The incredible rise in recent years of attorneys' starting salaries contribute to this image. So do derogatory lawyer jokes (What's the difference between a catfish and a lawyer? One's a scum-sucking bottom-dweller, and the other's a fish.) So do ads for lawyers who are commonly characterized as ambulance chasers ("Have you or anyone you know been hurt? You may be entitled to a large cash settlement. . . ."). High profile cases, like the O.J. Simpson trial and the McDonald's lawsuit for spilled hot coffee, don't help the image of lawyers either.

Surveys bear out the negative opinion most people have of lawyers. In 1993, the American Bar Association commissioned a comprehensive survey of public attitudes toward lawyers and the American legal system. It provided an interesting, and depressing, "snapshot" of lawyers as taken through the lens of the public eye. For instance, almost two-thirds of those surveyed said lawyers are greedy and that they make too much money. Fewer than a quarter thought the phrase "honest and ethical" describes lawyers, while nearly half of the respondents said that they felt that almost a third of lawyers lack the ethical standards necessary to serve the public. Fewer than one in five surveyed felt that the phrase "caring and compassionate" describes lawyers. And only about a third of the respondents said that lawyers are "a constructive part of the community." More than half said that lawyers are no longer leaders in the community, defenders of the underdog, or seekers of justice.

Lawyers don't fare much better when they're stacked up against other professionals. Those questioned in a 1990 survey were asked how much they trusted individuals in 11 occupations. Lawyers ranked eighth, after teachers, dentists, police officers, physicians, government workers, plumbers, and journalists. Only cab drivers, politicians, and car salesmen were trusted less than lawyers.

How does this affect you as an attorney? Frankly, on a day-to-day basis, when you're dealing with your clients and your colleagues, it doesn't affect you very much. For me, in an average day I'd only be speaking with the people I worked with, and my friends. In those kinds of situations public opinion polls don't matter much. But over time, it's true that your job becomes part of your identity. Derogatory lawyer jokes and under-the-breath comments you glean in social situations will inevitably affect the way you perceive your job and yourself. Never mind that lawyers aren't self-propelling, they only act on behalf of clients. And never mind that people feel entirely differently about lawyers, and large cash settlements, when they themselves feel that they've been wronged.

Their attitudes even change when they learn more about high profile cases; take the McDonald's spilled coffee case. If you ask most people what happened, they'll tell you that an old woman won millions of dollars from McDonald's when she spilled hot McDonald's coffee on herself. Who wouldn't be disgusted with a result like that—if that's all there was to it? But if you delve more deeply into the facts, you find that McDonald's had ignored hundreds of complaints from people about its coffee, which McDonald's itself acknowledged was scalding hot; knowing that most of its customers didn't drink the coffee right away, it deliberately served blistering coffee to ensure that the coffee would be hot when customers *did* get around to drinking it. Furthermore, the old woman in question underwent several painful operations to treat the burn, some of which required skin grafts. And finally, her actual settlement was reduced on appeal to a tiny fraction of the original jury award. All of a sudden a lawsuit that seemed outrageous in tabloid headlines becomes more reasonable. And it becomes even more reasonable if you put yourself in the woman's shoes and ask yourself what you'd expect *your* lawyer to do on your behalf. Nonetheless, those kinds of misperceptions are part of what you have to learn to deal with when you become a lawyer.

September 9

Today Laura told me a story that epitomizes the bulls**t that gets thrown around when firms attempt to attract new recruits.

Laura was in Jim's office talking with Jim [a partner] about a book that she's editing for him. While they were talking, Shelly, Jim's secretary, said that Scott Burrows was on the phone.

Scott is a law school recruit who interviewed with Jim a few weeks ago. Apparently, as part of his recruiting spiel, Jim had told Scott that he would love to discuss Scott's law review article with him. Scott bought into it and called today to take Jim up on his offer.

With Laura still there, Jim put Scott on speakerphone and greeted him with enthusiasm. They talked briefly about how Scott was doing at law school and then moved on to Scott's article. Laura listened as Jim launched into endless praise of the note, extolling the virtues of the approach that Scott had taken. Scott took Jim's praise and ran with it.

As Scott droned on about all the theories and arguments he rejected while drafting the article, Jim momentarily dropped his recruiting hat to show Laura it was all just an act to make Scott feel warm and fuzzy about the firm—he turned to Laura, picked up

Scott's note between his thumb and index finger, hung it over the garbage pail, and dropped it in.

But it got better. A moment later, Jim paused and seemed to rethink his actions, as if he had gone too far and had experienced sudden regrets. He reached down into the garbage pail, pulled out Scott's article, saved the paper clip, and then dropped the article back in.

While a large firm's summer associate program will be its most visible recruiting tool, large firms, in fact, recruit "fresh blood" throughout the year. In the fall, the firms recruit first and second year students for summer positions, and third year students for permanent positions after they graduate the following May. In the spring, large firms focus on recruiting judicial clerks; that is, people who opted to work for judges after graduation, researching issues and writing opinions, instead of going straight into practice. These judicial clerkships typically last a year or two, after which the judicial clerks look for other jobs.

Law firms conduct two types of interviews when they recruit: "screening" interviews, and "call-back" interviews.

Screening interviews take place at law schools. Typically, large firms send attorneys to visit the "elite" law schools. A day interviewing students is grueling; it consists of 20-minute interviews, lasting from first thing in the morning until dinner time. As the name "screening interview" suggests, the purpose of the interview is to look at the initial pool of applicants to determine which of them should be called back to the firm's offices for further interviews.

Keep in mind that although these interviews are considered screens, a great deal of screening has already taken place in order to *get* to the screening interview. Because large firms are considered plum employers, they have the pick of top students at top schools. The vast majority of the 50,000-plus law students who graduate from law school every year simply don't have the credentials necessary to get even a screening interview. The ones who *do* know the kind of pressure they face—they've got 20 minutes in which to "connect" with the interviewer enough to get called back to the firm for further interviews. A personality clash with the interviewer, or simply an off-day, and the student's chances of working for a particular firm are dashed.

If a law student clears the screening interview hurdle, they'll get a so-called "call-back" interview at the firm's office. A call-back is basically a marathon interview, where the recruit meets with between four and seven attorneys for between 20 and 30 minutes each. After meeting with a recruit, each interviewing attorney will prepare a written evaluation of the recruit and forward it to the firm's recruiting coordinator. The recruiting coordinator, in turn, will turn the evaluations over to the firm's hiring committee, which will decide whether to make an offer to the recruit. No matter how many interviews are involved in a call-back, one bad interview can have a devastating effect on a recruit's chances of getting an offer from the firm, but generally only if it was a partner doing the interviewing. As a general rule, the younger the associate, the less influence a single interview—even a bad one—will have on the hiring process. Once a firm *does* extend an offer to a recruit, that offer will typically include a standing invitation to revisit the office and meet with other lawyers, and to learn more about the firm, if that's what they want to do.

Law students with great credentials can use the recruiting process as a real gravy train, because large firms pick up all of the student's expenses for out-of-town interviews. So if you are a top law student living in Los Angeles and you get invited back to a New York firm, your airfare, hotel bill, and all meals and incidentals will be picked up for you. One recruit told me a story about how she went to Atlanta on a call-back interview, and when she registered at the hotel, she mentioned the name of the firm that had made the reservation for her. The hotel clerk's face brightened, and he said, "Oh! Then you'll want to know about room service, and long-distance calls, and champagne. . . ." It's not unheard of for unscrupulous law students to charge up room service bills in the hundreds of dollars, knowing that the law firm will foot the bill.

Of course, picking up these kinds of costs are an advantage that large firms have over smaller firms, public interest groups, and government entities, which often have relatively small recruiting budgets. Large firms routinely spend half a million dollars a year recruiting new attorneys. That gives them the opportunity to wine and dine recruits in a manner no other kind of employer can top. It's a rare law student whose head isn't turned by this kind of kid glove treatment—and it typically means that large firms wind up with a lion's share of the "best" law students as associates.

September 30

I did my first recruiting lunch with Brad today.

Early this morning, Christine asked me whether I could have lunch with a recruit from Stanford Law School interviewing for a summer position. She mentioned that the lunch would be with Brad, and that she thought it might be good if someone else went along. I knew she didn't want to subject the poor guy to a one-on-one lunch with Brad.

My first instinct was to decline. Why risk getting more work from Brad by going to lunch with him? Then I realized that I was going to have to spend this morning with him anyway to prepare a witness for testimony in the Allegheny Industries case. I figured lunch probably wouldn't be that big of a risk since he'd have all morning to dump work on me. Besides, I had never seen Brad in a recruiting mode before and wanted to see him in action.

Brad, Mike, and I wrapped up the morning session with our witness at about 12:20 p.m., when Brad excused himself to make some calls. Christine had made 12:30 p.m. reservations at the restaurant where Brad usually takes clients and recruits to lunch, so I had 10 minutes to kill. I walked back to my office and then to the lobby, where Brad and I were meeting Steve, the recruit, for lunch.

Steve was waiting there when I arrived. As usual, Brad was running late, so Steve and I made small talk while we waited. A few minutes later, Brad walked briskly out of his office and joined us in the lobby. With his usual charming style, he introduced himself to Steve and apologized for being late.

Brad pushed the button to summon the elevator. A moment of awkward silence passed among us as we waited. Sensing the silence, Brad kicked into high gear by bluntly asking Steve whether he's on law review. Brad is obsessed with hiring only law students who are on law review. It's probably his main criterion for filtering through the hundreds of job applicants. Fortunately, Steve is on law review, so he maintained his viability and avoided a second awkward moment.

The three of us arrived at the restaurant and took our seats. Brad and I made some menu recommendations to Steve and then talked briefly about the work that I still need to do for Allegheny Industries. Of course, this was mostly for the benefit of Steve, who was supposed to believe that I have "significant responsibility" and regularly "work closely" with Brad. We ordered and then listened to Steve tell us about his background and interest in the law.

Lunch arrived a few minutes later, just as Brad began to make his recruiting pitch to Steve. As we ate, Brad explained his background and practice and the types of work that Steve might do if he were to join the firm. Like most other recruits, Steve nodded a lot and interjected an occasional question to make himself appear interested.

Brad began phase two by asking Steve which other firms he was considering. Steve gave a surprisingly honest answer, listing the names of four or five other firms. With this information, Brad proceeded to explain why Steve would ultimately find the work at each of the other law firms boring or too limiting. In just a few minutes, Brad had smoothly and effectively promoted our firm and bashed the competition.

Brad was on a roll, so I was pretty quiet during most of the lunch. I gave my 2¢ towards the end, when Brad put me on the spot by asking me how I liked working at the firm. I played along by describing only the best aspects of my job and saying that I enjoyed my work. I certainly wasn't about to jeopardize my job by denigrating the firm in front of Brad. But I probably would have "toed the firm line" even if Brad hadn't been there. I could give recruits nightmares with all the war stories I could tell, but I don't trust *them to keep things confidential, at least not after Frank Boyle got fired.*

Besides, the more recruits that actually join the firm, the less work I'll have to do. If they want the job, who am I to discourage them? Just because I'm not crazy about the job doesn't mean they won't be.

As a junior associate at a large firm, you're frequently pressed into service to provide a pleasant picture of the firm for potential recruits. Large firms do this as a means of providing a more balanced picture of the firm. After all, the work, perceptions, and lifestyles of partners and senior associates at the firm all differ radically from what a new associate faces.

That means that as a first year associate, you can expect to interview recruits in order to give them an idea of what their lives might be like if they joined the firm. Your firm may even encourage you to take recruits out to lunch, rather than interview them in the office, with the idea that a more social context outside the firm's confines will facilitate a more frank discussion. But no junior associate takes this notion of "frankness" too literally. Large firms don't want you to lie to recruits, but they *do* expect you to put a favorable spin on your description of the firm. For instance, if a recruit points out that your firm has a reputation for working longer hours than comparable firms, a response that "toes the firm line" would be that the longer hours result in bigger bonuses or a more prestigious reputation and, in turn, better legal work. If that's *not* true, and you really do work in a sweatshop with nothing to show for it, your firm would expect you to avoid the subject, or, alternatively, minimize discussion of it. When recruits asked me about the hours I worked, I generally said that I *did* work long hours, but I also pointed out that all firms—large or small—require their lawyers to work long hours if there's work in the office to be done. I would go on to tell them that they were kidding themselves if they thought a smaller firm would require fewer hours of them for quality-of-life concerns. I'm still confident that that *does* happen once in a blue moon, but I've never heard of any firm, large or small, turning down work because it already has too much.

Like every other attorney at your firm, as a junior associate you evaluate every recruit you interview, and offer your opinion on whether or not the firm should make the recruit an offer. While your evaluation carries less weight than that of a partner or senior associate, it *is* used to help determine how well a particular recruit would fit in at the firm. In fact, recruit evaluations are one of the few instances where your candid comments regarding office management are welcomed by your firm.

As a junior associate, you'll find that interviewing recruits has its pros and cons. On the plus side, interviewing potential coworkers is one of the few ways that you can have an impact on your work environment, since you spend most of your waking hours either working or socializing with your colleagues. Interviewing also gives you a chance to dine at fine restaurants, courtesy of the firm, since most large firms encourage you to treat recruits to expensive meals. On the occasional day when your workload is light, a free lunch at a expensive restaurant is a great perk.

But interviewing recruits has its downside, as well. For one thing, because it's not billable to any client, the time you spend interviewing recruits cuts into your precious leisure time. And sometimes the interviewees themselves are simply downright unpleasant. My own experience, and that of virtually everybody I worked with, was that there's a contingent of law students who are simply arrogant, and displaying arrogance is one of the fastest ways to get yourself eliminated from contention by a law firm. Remember, no matter how good your credentials are, virtually *everybody* at large firms has excellent credentials, as well.

Whether an interviewee is undesirable due to arrogance or any other character flaw, there's nothing worse than finding yourself wasting time on an extended interview lunch when it's clear from the outset that there is no "fit" between the recruit and your firm. A friend from another firm told me about a recruit he had to take to lunch. The recruit in question was a young woman with great credentials, but no personality at all. Within the first 5 minutes of the lunch, he had asked all of the questions he could think of, and, in his words, "Not only didn't she pick up the conversational ball, all she did was grunt." Not exactly the way *anybody* wants to spend their time, especially a harried junior associate!

October 13

I had a bad night tonight.

I realized I was running late at about 9:15 p.m., as I was leaving my apartment. I hopped in my car—a Porsche 944—and drove over to Rob's house. Rob was waiting outside for me when I pulled up. He got in, and we drove over to Laura's and Sara's apartment to pick them up before heading to the movies. Rob and I just wanted to stop in for a few minutes, but we still had to park. As usual, all the street spaces were taken.

We finally decided to park in a lot about 20 yards away from Laura's and Sara's building. The lot was clearly for residents of the apartment building, but the spaces weren't reserved and we didn't see any signs telling us not to park there. We'd be gone for just a few minutes anyway.

Fifteen minutes later, the four of us walked toward the empty parking space that formerly held my car. My car had been towed! We looked around and saw a small metal sign posted about 20 feet away saying "No Parking. Cars towed by J & J Towing." There was a phone number at the bottom, but Laura knew where the towing company's storage lot was because another one of her friends had recently made the same mistake. Sensing I was about to lose it, Laura offered to drive us to the storage lot.

I was furious. I felt like a nuclear reactor that was about to have a meltdown. During the drive to the storage lot, the only way I could control my anger was to remain silent. I knew I'd explode if I spoke, and I had no reason to yell at Rob, Sara, or Laura.

Laura pulled up to a trailer that was parked in the lot. I jumped out and walked quickly to the front of the trailer. I was ready to kill. As I approached the trailer, I saw a large Hispanic man in a black leather jacket extending his arm with a sheet of paper in it. I grabbed the sheet of paper from his hand, pointed my finger at him, and started screaming that my car shouldn't have been towed. The guy could have crushed me, but my adrenaline and testosterone levels were hitting record levels.

Despite my extended tirade, the man just stared at me blankly. He finally spoke.

"Eh? No hablo Ingles."

The synapses in my brain fired. His car had been towed too! We each thought the other worked for the towing company! I was floored momentarily, but didn't let that stop me. As Rob, Laura, and

Sara looked on in astonishment, I marched up the trailer stairs and started screaming through the trailer window at the woman inside. The woman and I fought ferociously as I paid the fine and got my car.

I definitely lost it tonight. I'm overworked and stressed to the max. I can usually put up a good front, especially at work, where I have to maintain a calm and professional exterior. But inside I feel like I'm always one step away from snapping, like a bomb ready to explode. In the storage lot tonight, I knew I could explode and still keep my job. So I did. Now my friends call me "Mr. Testosterone."

After practicing with the firm for about a year, my job was clearly taking its toll on me. Practicing law in the pressure-cooker environment of a large firm can cause a stress that makes your facial muscles tense, tie your back muscles in knots so tight you get backaches, and make you snap at people you work with and care about.

And it can make you think that it's just not worth it.

Where does the stress come from? One of the vexing things about it is that you can't attribute it to just one source. For most lawyers, job stress comes from a variety of factors that pile on and compound one another. While your own personality, tolerance, and work environment will determine how stressed out you become, you're likely to encounter at least some of the sources of stress that most junior associates face.

The most obvious stress-producer is overwork. Like most attorneys, you'll probably strive to complete quality work, on time. But if you're constantly faced with too much work, you'll find yourself constantly playing catch-up, always just slipping in under the wire. You may be nagged by doubts about your ability to meet your next deadline.

You may be plagued with questions about whether your rushed work-product is up to snuff.

It's ironic that a job that makes you miserable can stress you out even more if you're worried that you may not be able to hang onto it. A traditional lure of large firms was that they provided lawyers with a sense of economic security and employment stability. However, as law firms have become more like corporations, they have focused more closely on the bottom line, taking whatever steps necessary to stay competitive and profitable. As a result, they've been more willing to cut partners and associates in order to cut expenses and improve the firm's bottom line—even if those dismissed lawyers were perfectly competent. As a young lawyer in a large firm, this creates a "survival of the fittest" mentality that stretches your nerves even more taught.

A more predictable source of stress is the adversarial and hostile work environment lawyers face. Think about what lawyers do: they confront and solve other people's problems. On a daily basis, they have to deal with actual or threatened litigation, tense negotiations, posturing, and hostile phone calls. If you're a litigator—like I was—who is hired to fight a client's legal battles, you'll find yourself living in the most adversarial environment possible. While the battle eventually ends for your clients as their problems are resolved, you, as a litigator, remain in a constant state of conflict. You move from battle to battle, often becoming insensitive and combative along the way as a means of coping.

A friend from law school told me about an experience of hers that highlighted the mental callousness that large-firm lawyers often develop to cope with their jobs. As a summer clerk, she had had to work on a case where a teacher was fired and her firm's client, the school board, had to justify the firing. As my friend researched the case further, she found that the teacher had, in fact, been unjustly fired. The first time my friend got to actually see this teacher was at a hearing before an arbitrator, and she was terribly upset to find that the woman was truly devoted to her job—warm and kind, and exactly the kind of person who *ought* to be teaching. My friend realized that if her firm was successful, this woman would lose her job and probably be blackballed from the teaching profession. And if that happened, it would be at least in part due to the research she'd done on the school board's behalf. This experience made my friend reconsider her career in law, although she half-heartedly went on a couple of law firm interviews after her summer clerkship. At one of these interviews, she recounted the teacher case to a junior associate. He stared at her blankly and said, "You mean that *bothered* you?" As my friend told me, "I wasn't so bothered by the fact that this guy reacted the way he did, but by the notion that if I took a job at that firm, *I'd* turn out that way—I'd have to steel myself like he had done." Needless to say, she didn't pursue that career.

It's difficult to imagine, without personal experience, just how harrowing the life of a litigator can be. Here is a portion of a transcript from a pretrial deposition from a lawsuit a couple of years ago. The suit itself alleged that Monsanto Company had exposed residents of Houston to dangerous chemicals. (Incidentally, a deposition is a kind of minitrial, where people who are likely to testify at the trial itself are questioned by lawyers for the opposing party.) The excerpt features an exchange between two top litigators, Joseph Jamail and Edward Carstarphen:

> *Jamail:* You don't run this deposition, you understand?

Carstarphen: Neither do you, Joe.

Jamail: You watch and see. You watch and see who does, big boy. And don't be telling other lawyers to shut up. That isn't your g**damned job, fat boy.

Carstarphen: Well, that's not your job, Mr. Hair-piece.

Witness: As I said before, you have an incipient —

Jamail: What do you want to do about it, a**hole?

Carstarphen: You're not going to bully this guy [the witness].

Jamail: Oh, you big tub of s**t, sit down.

Carstarphen: I don't care how many of you come up against me.

Jamail: Oh, you big fat tub of s**t, sit down. Sit down, you fat tub of s**t.

This isn't the kind of exchange litigators engage in every day—and, in fact, Jamail and Carstarphen crossed a line that most attorneys won't cross, no matter how stressed out they are. What it *does* show, however, is a worst case scenario of the stress level at which some attorneys work, and the unfortunate situations that sometimes arise in extreme adversity.

Lawyers who strive to *avoid* the appearance of conflict often find the act of avoidance stressful, as well. As a lawyer, you must typically suppress your natural aggressive instincts, and keep a calm, controlled composure in tense, stressful, and hostile situations. This, in and of itself, produces stress. So lawyers who *aren't* able to vent their aggression in an adversarial environment may find themselves stressed as a result.

Dr. Gary Lefer, a respected psychiatrist who has studied lawyer stress extensively, believes that a change in the law firm environment over recent years has added to the misery of lawyers. He points out that in the old days, law firms functioned more like "clubs," with the attorneys feeling like "part of a closely knit group with a common purpose. The law firm . . . served as a kind of family unit." However, over time, Dr. Lefer has watched the law firm evolve into an entirely different kind of animal. He sees modern law firms as "too large and too hierarchical to function as clubs." Rather than being a "safe house" for lawyers, the firms have become "battlegrounds. Junior partners vie for position; senior partners find themselves thrust into unfamiliar roles as managers or account executives, tending to the business rather than the practice of law." Dr. Lefer cites the increasing specialization of lawyers as smashing the "common goal" feeling of old law firms. This leaves lawyers feeling isolated, and "these stresses are compounded by the isolation that is often associated with the corporate environment. This alienation may be further deepened by separation from family and from support groups such as the church, the synagogue, or community organizations imposed by the demands of the job."

How do lawyers cope with all of this stress? Unfortunately, law's dirty little secret is that many lawyers turn to alcohol for solace. They find the numbing effect of a scotch—or a few scotches—relaxes and "loosens them up." Lawyers are confronted with constant temptations to drink, at firm parties, receptions, and client and recruiting lunches and dinners.

Imagine working as hard as you can possibly work. Then imagine drinking a six-pack of beer or six cocktails *every day*, and *still* trying to get all your work done. Sound inconceivable? According to a 1990 survey by the American

Bar Association, one out of every eight lawyers drinks that much! A survey conducted by the *International Journal of Law and Psychiatry* determined that while one out of ten American adults are alcoholic, the number of lawyer alcoholics may be almost double that. Perhaps there is no greater indication of the stress associated with practicing law than the fact that the rate of alcoholism for practicing attorneys is almost double that for the general population.

For those who stick with practicing law, the statistics on alcoholism get even more depressing. A Washington State study showed that of lawyers who had practiced 20 years or more, one out of four had a drinking problem.

Maybe you're thinking, "Statistics are just numbers. *I* won't become an alcoholic." Most alcoholics used to think the same thing. And even if you don't turn to drink, you may find yourself—as I started to do—questioning more and more whether you've made the right choices with your career.

November 1

I realized today that I'm not getting as much experience from my job as I could or should be getting.

Alex, my high school buddy, called me from California this afternoon just to catch up and say hello. As we were talking, he told me he took his first deposition a few days ago [a deposition takes place before trial; essentially it gives lawyers a chance to question the other side's witnesses]. I was more than a little surprised that he was taking a deposition since he's a first year associate, too. I blurted out, "You don't mean by yourself, do you?" He said "yeah," noncha-

lantly, and went on to explain how the opposing lawyer gave him a hard time during the depo.

I tried to explain to Alex that taking a deposition isn't even a possibility for me. I told him I'll be lucky if I get to watch one being taken by one of the partners. He sympathized, but he's at a regional, medium-sized firm, and I don't think he really understands the way my firm works. Young lawyers in my firm rarely get any real responsibility because the stakes are simply too big. Besides, we're on the bottom of a tall totem pole—there's plenty of more senior associates who get first dibs on depositions and court appearances.

What still amazes me is the level of anxiety that Alex's off-the-cuff comment aroused in me. I got a sudden sinking feeling in my stomach as I realized that while I'm wasting time reviewing documents, researching and writing memos all day, first year associates at other firms are getting real litigation experience.

What really bothers me is that these are the very years that I'm supposed to be learning and making mistakes. How am I supposed to learn if I never get the chance? What will it be like as a fifth year associate making the mistakes that Alex made as a first year? I'm getting paid a lot, but I'm not learning to think on my feet or act like a lawyer. I'm afraid I'm getting passed by.

Everybody who considers working at a large firm has heard horror stories about associates who spent years at large firms, grinding out research and being bit players in very large cases, only to be shut out of becoming a partner, and finding themselves with few skills that are marketable to any other kind of employer. During my day-to-day life at the firm, I never really thought about that. But conversations like this with old friends, gave me my first real feelings of unease about working for a large firm—showing me, as they did, how I could have far more control over my life if I worked elsewhere. This feeling, however, didn't overwhelm me. Not yet, anyway.

The mention of depositions is as good a place as any to introduce you to the methods of "discovery" you'll face if you become a litigator. "Discovery" covers many of the things that happen before a case gets to trial; in essence, it's the process of "discovering" what the facts of a case are. As a litigator, you quickly learn that real life isn't anything like Perry Mason; you just don't get the surprises in court that you see on TV. And that's because of the discovery process. Ideally, by the time you get to court, you know all the evidence, and what all of the witnesses are going to say, because discovery gives you a chance at a kind of "dress-rehearsal" beforehand.

There are a lot of different methods of discovery. Depositions are a popular one; another frequently used discovery method is interrogatories.

In a deposition, lawyers for one side get to question an opposing party or a witness for the opposing party, in a kind of minicourtroom setting; lawyers for both sides are present, the witness has to take an oath to tell the truth, and the questioning is a lot like it would be in court. There's even a court reporter to record the deposition and prepare a verbatim account of the proceedings in the form of transcripts. Lawyers typically purchase these transcripts to help them prepare for trial, or to help them reach a settlement with the other side.

With all of the people who have to be present, you might think that a deposition would be very expensive to conduct. And it *is*, especially if the firm handling the deposition is a large one, with high hourly rates. But depositions are far and away the most useful pretrial device. Watching a skilled litigator conduct a deposition is like watching a surgeon perform delicate surgery. Through artful questioning, it's possible to trick or force the person testifying (who's called the "deponent") into admitting liability or negligence, make a major concession, or establish one or more element of your own client's case. With such statements in hand, you can extract a favorable settlement or impeach the deponent's credibility if (s)he testifies at trial.

Unfortunately, as a junior associate at a large firm, it's unlikely that you'll get to take part in a deposition, since that's almost always left to senior attorneys with litigation experience. During the time I spent with the firm, I never took or even sat in on a deposition. So even though, as a junior associate at a large firm, you get to practice in the presence of great attorneys, you don't get the kind of hands-on experience that you might relish.

As a junior associate you probably *will* get to prepare and respond to interrogatories, the other popular form of discovery. Unfortunately, interrogatories aren't nearly as interesting as depositions. Interrogatories are written questions posed to a party, witness, or anyone else with a connection to the case. The person who receives the questions has to write answers to them.

Of course, it isn't really the party to the case who writes the questions or the answers to interrogatories; it's the firm who's representing that party. So if you're representing the party seeking the information, you're the one who drafts the questions necessary to get that information. You'll want to phrase the questions carefully in order to obtain the information you need, and that's no simple task. The difficulty is that when you're formulating interrogatories, you aren't sure what the facts *are*, so it's sometimes impossible to know how to elicit the information you want.

Conversely, if you represent the party who receives the interrogatories, you're saddled with preparing truthful but strategic responses, with your client helping out. You want to reveal as little information as possible to your opponent while staying within ethical boundaries—you've got to act in good faith. That can involve some intellectual acrobatics, but it's not terribly stimulating. In fact, most litigators find interrogatories tedious. I was lucky enough not to have to deal with interrogatories while at my firm. But knowing that lawyers my own age at other, smaller firms were getting real experience, was starting to eat away at me.

December 5

It's Sunday night and I'm bitter. I spent the whole damn weekend working in the office on the Allegheny Industries case. Last night, I was there until 10:00 p.m.

Actually, I'm not bitter because I had to work the whole weekend. I don't mind working hard. In fact, I prefer to work hard as long as I believe that I'm accomplishing or producing something valuable and important. The problem is, I rarely feel that way at work. I've done little or no "sophisticated" legal work, and hardly any work that I've actually been interested in.

I've always got a ton of work to do, but it's so damn boring. I was bored out of my skull on Friday, when I forced myself to become a glassy-eyed drone and churn out some billable hours. Sometimes I get so bored that I wonder how I'm going to make it through the afternoon, let alone the week, the year, the decade. I can't believe I could conceivably spend the rest of my life practicing law.

I've been thinking a lot lately about whether I can do something else for a living. I don't even need to make the kind of money I'm earning. I'd rather have my life back. I just want a good salary that will let me live my life without worrying about money everyday. It's not like I don't want to be successful. I do. I just want to be successful at something I actually like doing—or at least that I don't dislike doing. Why is that such a problem?

As my diary shows, by the time I approached the end of my first year at the firm, I was seriously questioning my career choice. I wasn't alone in second-guessing myself; job dissatisfaction is a serious problem plaguing the legal profession. More and more, lawyers are questioning whether the rewards of their jobs outweigh—or even justify—the stress, personal sacrifices, and unwavering dedication that accompany those rewards. The increasingly common answer to that is "no," as lawyers change careers in record numbers.

I know that from the outside looking in, it's tough to feel sorry for people in their mid-twenties with prestigious jobs, earning upwards of a $100,000 a year—no matter *how* many sacrifices they make and how many hours they work. After all, investment bankers, accountants, doctors, and other professionals also "live to work," routinely putting in 60 to 100-hour workweeks, including weekends. It's possible for *any* professional to lead a full and happy life if they enjoy their work and find it fulfilling. Conversely, you can be happy even if you don't find your work fulfilling; many blue-collar workers don't enjoy their work, but because they work shorter workweeks, they have enough leisure time to enjoy their personal and social lives, which compensates them for what they *don't* get from their jobs.

But many large-firm lawyers have the worst of both worlds, as I did: I lived to work and I didn't find that work fulfilling. As a lawyer you've got to do what your clients need done, but it will rarely involve anything you find genuinely interesting. A colleague of mine at another firm, who did corporate work, said to me, "I wouldn't find a prospectus interesting under the *best* of circumstances. At 3 o'clock in the morning, when I'm at some printer waiting for the damn thing to be printed, it's the last thing I want to read."

Some professionals can rationalize the sacrifices they have to make now by looking down the road, at the long-term benefits they can reap from their labors. But I found, as many junior associates do, that that doesn't work too well in a large firm. It takes 8 to 10 years to make partner in a big firm, but due to tough competition and few partnership openings, there's no guarantee that if you put in the time, you'll become partner. That makes it difficult to relate your daily activities to the ultimate goal of partnership. Even if you *can*, partnership may be no panacea. A 1990 study by the American Bar Association showed that almost a quarter of male partners at law firms are dissatisfied with their jobs, and almost half of female partners feel the same way. Hating what you do now, and unable to see any long-term payoff for it, you're likely to find resentment creeping into your inevitable neglect of personal relationships, hobbies, and interests.

You might be asking yourself why I didn't foresee that my work would be unfulfilling. After all, I spent 3 years in law school, and then I spent 3 months in my firm's summer associate program before coming in as a permanent associate. Shouldn't I have been wise to what I was in for?

Unfortunately, I wasn't, and I don't think many people *are.* Most people in law school—and even those contemplating going to law school—are high-minded, envisioning themselves as using the legal system to right social wrongs, further just causes, and otherwise contribute to society. Law school encourages these lofty ideals by encouraging you to provide *pro bono* (free) legal services and represent the poor and needy. In law school, your work and your idealistic pursuits become indistinguishable.

When you enter the real world of big-firm practice, however, you find those goals difficult, if not impossible, to achieve. Most large firms claim that they'll give you opportunities to do *pro bono* work, but in fact their attention to the bottom line means those opportunities are limited or nonexistent. Let's face it—those $100,000 salaries have to be paid by *someone,* and it's not indigents. As a result, your clients are often huge corporate institutions rather than oppressed people trying to stand up for their right. In fact, you're more likely to represent the *oppressors* than the oppressed since they're the ones with the money to pay the huge legal fees large firms demand. You will be fighting to make rich clients richer. Your work will be boring and your hours will be long. In short, you'll find that the practice of law isn't what you envisioned at all.

Before I practiced law, I also had a vision many law students share, of being able to perform free legal work for friends, family, and community organizations after work and on weekends. Unfortunately, this wasn't the case, even if there was the time to do it. That's because associates at most firms, particularly large firms, agree to perform legal work only for their firms' clients. If you want to do *pro bono* legal work for people or organizations who aren't clients, you need to get permission from your firm's management committee. This policy is based on the necessity of avoiding conflicts of interest, as well as the law firms' belief that any legal work performed by their salaried associates should be on behalf of one of their clients. In short, they bought your legal services and you can't give them away—even to your family.

Maybe you think you can put up with all of these pitfalls because you've got your eye on the immediate prize—the huge salary junior associates get. That reminds me of a famous quote from Orson Welles in the movie *Citizen Kane*, where, as Charles Foster Kane, he said, "It's not difficult to make a lot of money, if money is all you want." But if you're honest with yourself, you realize it's *not* all you want. I soon discovered that no amount of income, prestige, or professional pride can adequately compensate you if you believe your legal career is damaging your personal relationships and ruining your life. The high salary, large expense accounts, and chauffeured sedans waiting to whisk you to airports and meetings sound glamorous, but they quickly become meaningless, and, worse, you begin to resent them as representing the very things you feel are wrong with your life.

December 16

It's 1:00 a.m., and I was on the brink tonight. I almost quit.

I've been up to my neck in work from the Allegheny Industries case for the last few weeks, but it's been crazy the last couple of days. We've been interviewing company personnel and getting ready for our big presentation to the federal government on Monday.

This afternoon, Brad, Mike, and I were meeting with Gary Beck, Allegheny's former Chief Financial Officer, and his lawyer to pick their brains and help us prepare for our presentation. When the meeting ended at 5:30 p.m., Mike and I followed Brad into his office for a follow-up conference.

Brad, Mike, and I talked a little about Beck's role in the case before we started discussing the best strategy for finishing all the work that needs to get done by Monday morning. Brad thought that I should prepare the written portion of the presentation myself while Mike worked with Beck to learn more about Allegheny's complicated and unusual accounting system.

Mike and I knew this was a terrible approach. We both knew the presentation still needs a tremendous amount of work. Even with both of us working through the weekend, we'd barely finish it in time. Besides, I didn't want to do all the work myself, and Mike didn't want me to try since he's responsible for supervising me and managing the case. We argued with Brad for a few minutes, but he was being fairly insistent.

Frustrated, Mike erupted. "Brad, you can't just lock Bill in a room and expect him to walk out on Monday with the finished presentation." Brad returned a slightly puzzled look that seemed to say "Why not?" before shrugging his shoulders, giving in, and saying we could work together on the presentation. He apparently realized that he was viewing the case from 30,000 feet and that we were the ones on the ground doing the work. I left Brad's office having realized a simple truth: Brad doesn't give a s**t about me, as long as I get the work done.

I had a full night's work ahead of me (despite Brad's change of mind) and returned to my office. As if things weren't bad enough, Brad called me at about 8:00 p.m. and dumped more work on me. When I got off the phone, I slumped down in my chair, over-

whelmed with work. I felt like I was being buried alive and wished I were someone else.

At about 11:30 p.m., I was in the office by myself. I was tired, frustrated, bitter, and, most of all, fed up. Suddenly, the thought of quitting flashed into my mind. Just getting up and walking out. That would show them, I thought. I was so angry and miserable that I was certain I'd never regret just getting out and saving myself. I got out of my chair and paced the silent, empty hallways for a few minutes. It was incredibly liberating—and cathartic—to contemplate the profound effect that the two simple words "I quit" could have on my life.

Then, I got a grip. I knew I was much too tired to be thinking rationally. I decided I would show up for work tomorrow and then decide whether to quit. I packed up my things and called a chauffeured sedan to take me home.

Now that I'm in the comfort of my own home, I've decided not to quit, at least not in the next couple of days, no matter how bad it gets. I don't want to leave my first job as an attorney on bad terms. Besides, it'll be a lot easier to get a new job while I still have this one.

But they're starting to draw blood.

I was obviously getting to the end of my rope with my job, but fortunately my thoughts didn't venture beyond quitting. Many lawyers' reactions to dissatisfaction with their jobs is much worse. Researchers in North Carolina found that more than one in ten attorneys in the state thought of taking their lives at least once a month. According to the *International Journal of Law and Psychiatry,* about one in five lawyers suffer from elevated levels of depression. A persistent down mood, a feeling of isolation, loss of the ability to experience pleasure and meaning in life, and physical symptoms like a loss of appetite, irregular sleep, and inactivity—these are the hallmarks of clinical depression. It's important to realize that getting over a case of depression isn't just a matter of putting on a happy face and "cheering up." It often requires professional counseling and/or drug therapy.

So, you may be wondering, why don't lawyers just quit and do something else? There are a number of reasons, perhaps none of them particularly satisfactory. But if you've ever endured a job you didn't like, you'll identify with some, if not all, of the reasons that keep miserable lawyers where they are.

For one thing, a lawyer who has been practicing in a specialty for many years may dislike his job intensely, but he will have developed an expertise and security in his ability to perform well. With little opportunity to develop a life outside of the profession, over time, lawyers often begin to define themselves *solely* by their work: "I'm a litigator" or "I'm a corporate lawyer." The prospect of giving up their career is tantamount to giving up the only identity they know.

Other dissatisfied lawyers put on blinders, and ignore their misery. As the researcher Don Itkin found, even lawyers who do recognize their unhappiness may feel unable to do anything about it, for a variety of reasons. Some feel trapped, believing that they just don't have viable options. Others blame themselves, feeling inadequate because they aren't living up to their career potential. And still others believe they have invested too much time and effort to leave the profession, having gone to law school for 3 years and sacrificed their personal lives for a number of years after that. You can see that the common thread is that many lawyers settle for secure dissatisfaction with a familiar situation, rather than face the discomfort and insecurity of change. In other words, it's a classic case of "the devil you know."

While the causes of clinical depression vary, psychologists believe that lawyers often become depressed by the inherent nature of some legal work. A 1995 *Wall Street Journal* article detailed some of the reasons for lawyer depression. For instance, many attorneys find their work too dull and detail oriented. Some lawyers, especially those specializing in narrow fields like tax, antitrust, and securities, find it difficult to feel passionate about "splitting hairs," the technical manipulation of words and concepts that their practices often require. For junior associates, especially, there is the frustration of toiling over memoranda and other work-product that often seems to disappear, unused and unneeded, into the void. A junior associate may work strenuously on a case for years without seeing its completion or any other definite results, which leads to tension and disillusionment. A feeling that you can't make a substantial impact on your environment no matter how hard you work deprives you of the power over your environment that psychologists believe is crucial to personal satisfaction.

The *Wall Street Journal* article further pointed out that the impact of practicing law on an attorney's self-perception and identity may also play a role in clinical depression. Attorneys who were drawn to the profession in the first place for idealistic reasons often discover that to be effective, they must distort their personalities by becoming pushy, aggressive, and contentious. Shy people who did well in law school may later be required to perform extroverted functions, like getting new clients and business, which they find excruciatingly difficult. In more severe circumstances, attorneys become so involved with their work that they begin to identify themselves with it. This identity loss can threaten an attorney's self-esteem, especially when the economy is bad, or their clientele changes, or they're feeling isolated within their law firm. Similarly, some attorneys internalize qualities that clients and potential clients project on them. Clients want a sharp-toothed shark as a lawyer, a quality that many lawyers readily internalize in order to maintain existing clients and attract new ones. For attorneys who grew up doing what was expected of them, practicing law can result in them performing distasteful deeds in order to continue doing what people want them to do.

Finally, the way senior attorneys treat junior associates can contribute to depression. Most young associates graduate from law school believing they will have at least some semblance of autonomy and authority in managing the cases they'll work on when they start to practice. As my own experience bears out, junior associates are almost always too inexperienced to make important case management decisions. Cut out of the decision-making loop, they are left feeling emasculated, dominated, and possibly even humiliated by seemingly omnipotent partners who tolerate little input. According to psychologists quoted in the *Wall Street Journal*, this "infantilization" by partners may connect young associates' work experience with childhood memories of parents, as well as with their childhood desire to please their parents and quell fears of abandonment.

I faced this "infantilization" firsthand. In one particularly blatant instance, a senior partner spent a very informative half-hour carefully explaining the approach he wanted a mid-level associate and me to use in a case. However, as he was gathering up his papers to leave, he casually mentioned that he had just spent "floor time" with us. Realizing that we probably wouldn't understand his comment because neither of us had children, he continued by explaining that "floor time" is time a parent spends on the floor with a small child, explaining concepts to the child on the child's level. Needless to say, these comments turned an otherwise positive experience into a degrading one.

Of course, not every lawyer becomes seriously depressed. Many don't; I didn't. But there are other, less serious reactions that are still very negative. One is a resort to materialism. Lawyers often believe that some things, like the type of law they practice, the long hours they put in, a bad marriage, and/or a lack of leisure time are beyond their control, or too difficult to change. One thing they can control is their often substantial income. All too often, these lawyers purchase expensive items with the substantial income *from* their jobs in an attempt to fill voids created *by* their jobs! These lawyers, believing that they're locked into jobs they hate, feel they deserve to enjoy the fruits of their labor. So they buy luxuries like expensive homes and cars—I drove a Porsche—and pay them off slowly over time. They either don't know, or don't want to know, that their purchases further "tighten the screws," binding them to jobs they can't stand. They're left with no choice but to stick with their jobs. They feel that any other equally well-paying job within the legal profession would just be more of the same, and that jobs outside the legal profession don't offer the same financial rewards. The more locked in they feel, the easier it becomes for them to rationalize buying another expensive item that further restricts their freedom. It's a vicious circle that few attorneys appreciate.

Regardless of the perception, there is, of course, a way out—to take some other job, even if it means sacrificing the prestige of being able to say you're a lawyer, and the financial perks that go along with it. In fact, a substantial number of large-firm attorneys quit between their second and sixth years. While many of them accept positions with smaller firms, corporations, and governmental agencies and branches, others, disgusted with practicing law in general, leave the profession entirely.

If you're in law school now, or considering law school, this dissatisfaction may be hard to believe. You may look at your own life and figure that you've made personal sacrifices before to get what you want and you don't have a problem with doing it again. Especially if you're in law school, considered a grueling experience in itself, you might think a large firm just *couldn't* demand more from you than law school does.

Well, it could. And it does.

Soon after you start practicing law at a large firm, you start confronting the issue of the price you're willing to pay to *be* a lawyer, on the partnership track, at a blue-chip firm. For the first year or so, your eagerness to succeed will act as an opiate, numbing you to the long hours and tedious work. But after that, you'll start thinking critically about your career and lifestyle.

That's what happened to me. For the first time, you find yourself questioning whether your career is truly the highest priority in your life. You may confront questions you've never asked yourself before. What are my goals? Why did I choose those goals? Would I have a better marriage, or better relationship, if I worked less? Do I really want to earn as much money as possible? If so, at what price? Would I trade a high salary for more leisure time? Have the luxuries I coveted brought me the pleasure I thought they would? Do I spend money to reward myself for hard work, thereby perpetuating a vicious cycle? Am I materialistic, and, if so, did I become that way to fill a void in my life?

It wasn't until I'd been at the firm for a year that I was able to answer these questions in a meaningful way. Before that, I simply couldn't envision what a job like mine would actually be like to live with day after day. Even as a summer associate, it's difficult to perceive the day-to-day grind with anything approaching clarity. It wasn't until I actually lived with the hours, the stress, and the tedium day in, day out, week in, week out, that I that I began to feel the nagging sensation that maybe—just maybe—it wasn't worth it.

January 3

I became a second year associate today. It won't make a difference in my daily life, but at least I get a $15,000 raise. It's all for the money.

I'm not really sure where my career is heading, but I've resigned myself to sticking around for another year. That way, I can say I did the New York law firm thing for 2 years. The first year was so disappointing, though—I can't stand the thought of staying another year. Maybe it will go as fast as the first 15 months. Maybe it'll take me that long to work up the nerve to actually leave.

I just hope I don't keep wishing my life away.

January 14

Something very disturbing happened today.

Late this afternoon, Rob called me to tell me that Susan would be joining us for drinks after work. Susan is a third year law student working at the firm between classes to offset some of her tuition bills. She occupies a unique position in the firm because she's neither a summer associate nor a full-time associate. Her part-time status lets her experience the harsh realities of large-firm practice, while still letting her keep enough distance from the firm to retain her perspective on it. I told Rob I thought it was a great idea, not only because Susan would be fun to hang out with, but also because we could probably get reimbursed by the firm for "recruiting" Susan to become a permanent associate. Rob and I bulls****ed for a few minutes before making plans to meet Susan at the elevator bank and then walk over to a neighborhood bar where we were meeting several friends.

Part of the group was already at the bar when we arrived, so the three of us formed our own little clique and began gossiping about the firm. Before long, our conversation turned to Susan's experience at the firm, and I casually asked her whether she thought she might become a permanent associate after graduating from law school. I expected her to say "no" because she had already seen too much of the firm's innards, but her response nonetheless shocked me.

"I don't know," she said thoughtfully, couching her sincerity as politely as possible. "Everybody seems so unhappy."

Rob and I shot a glance at one another and then deflected her answer with laughter, a defense mechanism we had both adopted. The reality is that we have both been laughing at ourselves for so long that we have lost sight of the depravity of our situation. Neither of us is happy with our life or career choice, but we had no idea we were wearing our discontent on our faces. Susan's observation *brought home to us that we didn't even realize how unhappy we were.*

The rest of the evening passed quickly, but Susan's comment continued to disturb me even on the train home tonight. As I stared out the window, I wondered why I, and so many of my colleagues, were so unhappy. Objectively we have everything—we work at a prestigious law firm, earn top pay even among lawyers, own nice homes, drive expensive cars. Yet unhappiness hangs like a dark cloud over us.

I know I've developed a distaste for practicing law. How did I get this unhappy?

What Susan saw in our faces was a reflection of not just one problem, but a myriad of factors that meshed into a lifestyle that was inescapably oppressive. The cumulative effect of serving the firm with blind loyalty around the clock, working in an environment in which I had little control, and feeling like I was "selling out" for a paycheck and title were weighing ever more heavily on me. I felt trapped.

What I found most disturbing about Susan's comment was that it took a virtual stranger to point out my own unhappiness. Caught in the daily grind of firm life, I never even thought to question whether I was happy, because I was *supposed* to be happy. Why, I'd achieved a level of success that society has traditionally encouraged, one that most parents dream about for their children. Questioning whether I was happy meant questioning all the hard work, schooling, commitment, and money I had invested over the years to become a "successful lawyer." The task was made all the more difficult by the tremendous social pressure I felt to refrain from "throwing away" everything I had achieved. Most of all, and perhaps even more frightening, questioning my happiness meant questioning my very identity. For years, I thought I knew exactly what I wanted, and believed I was destined to become a top attorney. Questioning those long-held beliefs meant reevaluating not just my long-term goals, but also my sense of who I was. I was reminded of a story from the Russian Revolution. The last Russian czar, Nicholas II, abdicated in 1917. He had been hated by the Russian peasantry, but when one peasant found out that Nicholas was gone, she said that he might have been bad, but *now* they had nothing. Life outside of my firm had become an abyss, and I knew it would summon whatever courage I had to make the jump.

February 15

I had quite a revelation while skiing at Lake Tahoe today.

While riding the ski lift up the mountain together, Allison [a college friend and a nurse] and I were joking and catching up with one another. About halfway up the mountain, we started talking about our jobs and she asked me what it's like to be a lawyer. I wasn't sure how to answer, so I started telling her about the Allegheny Industries case. Without identifying the company or the people involved, I explained that I'm defending a corporation and its employees in a government investigation. I also mentioned that a company officer may have committed fraud and will probably confess later in the investigation. I thought she'd be impressed, but she surprised me by asking, "Why would you want to defend somebody like that?"

She caught me off guard. I didn't have a good answer, but I deflected the question by saying something to the effect that everyone is entitled to representation. I knew, however, that Allison was not questioning the merits of the American judicial system. She wanted to know why I'm spending my life defending individuals and companies whose conduct I sometimes find repugnant. In essence, she asked me why I'd "sold out."

The sad truth is, I don't know why. In fact, I didn't even realize I'd sold out.

Before I ever became a lawyer, I both respected and was intrigued by lawyers' ability to put their personal beliefs aside and zealously advocate positions they themselves didn't support. Rather than perceiving lawyers as prostitutes of their legal skills, I saw their ability to defend seemingly indefensible positions as the purest form of advocacy. In some ways, I still respect that skill. But now I recognize that separating yourself from your work comes at a high price. The lawyer in the office for 12 or more hours a day is the same person who has to go home each night, and live with the consequences of their actions.

The nature of large firm practice often masks the harsh reality of selling out. As a general rule, as an associate you are expected to work on cases assigned to you, unless you have—and can articulate—very strong moral or ethical objections. This pressure means that associates must take a stand to get off cases they don't want to work on, and that's a potentially career-jeopardizing move. It leaves people looking down on you for not being a "team player." Although I was never so repulsed by a client or case that I felt compelled to make such a stand, I lived with the very real possibility of having to represent clients I'd rather avoid. What makes turning an assignment down on moral or ethical grounds even more difficult is the sophistication and luxurious trappings of the firm. Surrounded by other professionals who routinely put their personal beliefs aside, and surrounded by plush offices, expensive artwork, and state-of-the-art technology, I found it depressingly easy to overlook any distaste I harbored for certain clients and cases.

Ironically enough, even though my legal education had supposedly taught me how to think logically, at the same time it impeded my ability to think introspectively and focus on how I felt. Law schools tend to emphasize a linear thought process in order to form coherent arguments, so that arguments flow naturally from the arguments that precede them. That was great for thinking logically, but it narrowed my thought process. It trained me to think within a set of prescribed parameters. I learned to juggle and think logically about difficult concepts, but I was horrified to discover, after I'd been at the firm for almost a year, that this came at the expense of my ability to open my mind to concepts and ideas of my own creation. Logical thinking had a profound effect on me. I virtually stopped questioning all that was not put before me. Because it was outside the four corners of my casework, I never stopped to ask myself whether my job impaired my personal integrity.

Until Allison's innocent question. *"Why would you want to defend somebody like that?"*

The answer: I *didn't* want to. That, by itself, wasn't enough to make me resign. But I realized that sooner or later—probably sooner—*something* was going to push me over the edge.

March 3

I've had it. This job is killing me.

Last Friday, I got a call from Rob at about 9:30 a.m. "Stay out of the hallways," he warned. "Scott's roaming the halls looking for people to work on Pinnacle's report to the Connecticut Insurance Department. Stay low—it's gonna be a lot of work. I just got nailed, so I'll stop by your office to talk about it in a few minutes."

Several months earlier, Pinnacle Insurance Corporation, one of the nation's largest insurance companies and among the firm's best clients, had undertaken a companywide compliance review in response to a crackdown by state insurance commissions on insurance sales practices. The review has been generating an enormous amount of work for the firm, but the work is among the worst to be had. Associates routinely run from it, and even Scott, who is Of Counsel, seemed to just grin and bear it. Scott specializes in securities laws, and you can sense that deep down, he hates insurance compliance work like the rest of us. Pinnacle is actually Brad's client, but Scott was filling in for Brad while Brad was on vacation in Florida with his family.

When Rob arrived, he explained that months earlier Brad had asked John, a junior partner, to take charge of the insurance commission's Request for Response—a questionnaire pertaining to insurance industry practices. John—and most insurance companies receiving the same questionnaire—believed that an appropriate response could be provided in a 10- to 50-page document. Thinking he and a few associates could crank out the response in a matter of days, John let the matter go until the last minute. Brad, however, had a different view. He never missed an opportunity to tell his client's story and saw this fairly routine response as a way to get on the insurance commission's good side by describing in detail every aspect of Pinnacle's compliance program. He wanted Pinnacle's response to be the definitive statement on insurance compliance, and a week ago yesterday, he directed Scott to assemble and supervise a team of lawyers responsible for preparing a lengthy report by yesterday. So on Friday morning, when Rob was telling me all of this, we both presumed that Scott had finished his associate round-up. The fact that Scott skipped over or missed me was sheer luck, because I couldn't have legitimately ducked the assignment if he had asked me to help out.

Twenty minutes later, I looked up from my work to find Scott, a solemn, 40-something lawyer, standing in my doorway. Without much of a greeting, he asked, "Can you fly up to Pinnacle today?" He spoke casually and quietly, as if the assignment was routine. I listed for Scott the cases I was working on, hoping he would assume I was too busy to go, but he was desperate for warm bodies. When I finished, he smiled knowingly and rather curtly said, "That stuff can wait. Why don't you get your things together and get on the next flight?" Realizing I didn't have a choice, I laughed a bit, shook my head, and said OK. When Scott left, I sat at my desk for a moment, mourned the loss of another weekend, and then called Rob to tell him that we would be working together.

By mid-afternoon, Rob and I arrived at Pinnacle's headquarters. We were immediately dispatched to different company divisions to interview company personnel and prepare a report section describing company policies and procedures intended to ensure legal compliance. My section was on Pinnacle's extensive training program for new agents and continuing education program for established agents. I had only a vague idea of what the report's structure and strategic approach would be at that point, but lacking any knowledge whatsoever about the training and continuing education program, I set out to assimilate the underlying background information, knowing that I would have to perform a follow-up interview and additional research. The two department heads I interviewed were cooperative and informative, but obviously frustrated by their need to hold an unscheduled 5½-hour meeting on a Friday night. We finished about 8:30 p.m., just as Rob was finishing up with his interviewees. We left the company's headquarters that night with a lot of information and agreed that we would be working at Pinnacle's headquarters through the weekend and probably longer. I couldn't help but think that Scott, with his casual, seemingly unknowing approach earlier that day, had sucker-punched me with the assignment.

A team of about 15 lawyers, comprised of Pinnacle's General Counsel, in-house counsel, and those of us from the firm, began Saturday with a 9:30 a.m. organizational meeting to coordinate the drafting process and discuss objectives and themes. Everyone appeared relaxed in their casual clothes, but their anxiety was soon revealed by the intensity of the ensuing discussion. Once we agreed on the report's true purpose and function, the meeting broke and we went our separate ways to begin our work. By that time, I had developed a much better understanding of the project's size and scope, but still had no idea how much pain and suffering lay ahead.

Hoping to complete a first draft by Sunday, we worked feverishly through Saturday so that our workload on Sunday wouldn't be unbearable. Each of us remained in our self-selected work areas, venturing out only to take much needed breaks and figure out whether our report sections would resemble each other enough in form and substance to produce a coherent whole. I was fortunate to find a semihidden office, and told only Rob and a few others where I was working. I was there to work and wanted to finish my section as soon as possible. The day passed surprisingly quickly, and the night even faster, as I discovered that organizing and presenting the information I had gathered the previous day was more time-consuming than expected. Rob and I shut down our computers at 3:30 a.m. and got back to the hotel a little before 4:00 a.m., tired but confident that we had made substantial progress.

Sunday morning began much the same way Saturday night ended, with the drafting process continuing at a swift pace. By Sunday afternoon, Scott had assumed the responsibilities of the report's initial editor and was sitting in a secretarial station editing the report sections that had then been completed. I put some finishing touches on my draft section, took a last look at it, and then gave it to Scott for his review. He unenthusiastically examined it in light of other sections he had reviewed before sending me away to fill in remaining gaps. Performing the same editorial services for the others, Scott kept the drafting process going into Sunday night.

Around 6:30 or 7 p.m., people started getting hungry and we ordered an unbelievable amount of food from a number of restaurants. I'm amazed at the amount of food we ate, and the voracious way we ate it. We were hungry, but we were doing more than eating. We had been cooped up for 2 weekend days, our noses to the grindstone, and we needed some sort of relief. With meals as the only justifiable break, we attacked our food—our only source of pleasure—with a vengeance. Then we grudgingly went back to work.

The work atmosphere remained rather subdued until about 8:30 p.m., with each of us battling fatigue and struggling to stay focused. Then the word got out. Pressured by Pinnacle's General Counsel, a long-time client, Brad was cutting short his vacation to review the draft report. The rumor was that he would be in around midnight, and that he was angry about having to return early from his vacation. Suddenly, there was renewed vigor in the air, as everyone applied slightly more scrutiny to their draft section in anticipation of Brad's senior-level review. Scott took charge of ensuring that everyone finished their sections, and he compiled the various parts so that Brad would be able to review some semblance of the whole report.

Brad arrived a little before midnight and said little as he made his way toward a large office near our primary work area. On his way into the office, he quietly asked Rob to follow him into the office. When Rob walked in, Brad shut the door and asked, "What the f**k is going on?" It was more or less a rhetorical question that allowed Brad to vent his frustrations before settling down to work. He was pissed, and he had a right to be. This seasoned attorney, who earns about a million dollars a year, and who had argued before the United States Supreme Court a number of times, had cut short his vacation with his family to edit a routine response to a state insurance commission. I realized then that his life was little better than mine, despite his income, experience, and partnership status.

After Rob's brief overview, Brad quickly set to work reviewing the 300-page document and began issuing commands to reorganize particular sections, insert additional points, and perform additional research. This process went on for about 3 hours, and, with few exceptions, Brad's comments went unquestioned. He was the senior partner, he was in charge, and it was late. While pleased with the report overall, he generated a substantial amount of additional work for those of us who had already been working all weekend.

Brad went home about 2:30 or 3 a.m., as soon as he finished reviewing the document. Others filtered out gradually as the hours passed. Rob and I regularly worked for Brad, and had an additional responsibility to ensure that progress on the document continued so that copies could be delivered to Pinnacle's key officers for review and comment as soon as possible. We, along with Tom, a third year associate, worked through the night and into Monday morning, making the necessary revisions. Between 7:30 and 8 a.m., people uninvolved with the project began reporting to work, the beginning of another week. The three of us, sporting dark circles under our eyes and still wearing casual clothes from the previous day, stood in stark contrast to those rested, well-dressed individuals and those who followed. When John joined us a little later he sent us back to our hotel to get some sleep.

Rob and I returned to work late Monday afternoon and joined a group of attorneys who had continued working on the document after our morning departure. The number of attorneys working full-time on the document had dwindled to about five by then, and progress came much slower. Contributing to our inefficiency were the frustrations and tensions that were developing rapidly among the mid- and junior-level attorneys. Much of the tension seemed to originate from a mid-level associate who seemed to think she was above insurance compliance work and late-night work, in part because she frequently spoke fondly of her days at Oxford as a Rhodes Scholar and at Harvard as a law student. By the time Monday evening became Tuesday morning, more than a few of us had begun snapping at each other and "going out for some air" to alleviate the tension.

We finally finished a draft of the document for review by company personnel at about 3:30 a.m. on Tuesday. Our work, however, was not yet done. We needed about 20 bound copies for distribution, and began copying them ourselves in the downstairs duplicating department so that they could be delivered first thing in the morning. There Rob and I were, wearing suits at 3:30 a.m., exhausted, frustrated, and delirious, struggling to operate copy machines that kept jamming every few minutes.

Later that morning, at 9:00, Rob and I met in the hotel lobby after just a few precious hours of sleep. We were both exhausted but knew there would be some "down" time while waiting for Pinnacle's lawyers and officers to provide us with feedback. The responses began coming slowly late Tuesday afternoon, but they soon began to overwhelm the group. To our dismay, reviewing the suggested revisions and incorporating the majority of them into the document proved extremely time-consuming, requiring us to work through Tuesday night and yesterday morning. As we worked through the night, we all fought bouts of temporary insanity. At about 6:30 yesterday morning, Tom grew so delirious that he became more of a liability than an asset. The turning point was when he set us back an hour by failing to save our word-processed document. I still remember him staring blankly at us when he told us he had forgotten to save it, as if the words were reverberating, unrecognized, in his head.

We continued working all day yesterday, when our limits were truly tested. Comments continued to flow in all day, even as our deadline approached, causing time-consuming revisions. Through-

out the afternoon, we kept modifying the report's text to incorporate comments, thinking they would be the last, and then checking and revising the page numbers in the extensive table of contents. We worked until 8:30 last night, when we sent the report to the print shop for reproduction and binding.

By that time, Rob and I were physically and mentally exhausted, having deprived ourselves of sleep for over 36 straight hours. We said little to each other as we walked back to the hotel, our minds clouded with fatigue, contemplating the ordeal we had just survived. Once we were in the hotel elevator, Rob looked at me, shook his head, and said, "You look like you're 35."

I looked at myself in the reflective elevator door and nodded in agreement. I'm 27.

Like every young professional, I realized that I had to "put in my time" before I could enjoy a lifestyle and career status I'd dreamed about. I recognized that this would mean developing my skills and earning a place for myself in the legal profession by performing routine, challenging work for a number of years. And I knew that lawyers aren't alone in this. Medical interns, for example, have to work 24-hour shifts while completing their residencies. People in a corporate setting must faithfully "climb the corporate ladder," learning office politics, and frequently finding their superiors taking credit for their work along the way. And salespeople must make countless cold calls, facing rejection on a steady basis.

As a law firm associate, the largest reward of your career—partnership—represents the proverbial carrot on the end of the stick. It's your deferred reward for investing years of hard work as a salaried employee. Until relatively recently, virtually all lawyers in private practice sought to become a partner, for the prestige, higher pay, fewer hours, and more interesting work they perceived going along with it.

Today, however, when law firms are profit centers run with a close eye on the bottom line, many young attorneys recognize that the carrot is attached to a much longer stick. Partnership today is viewed as "more of the same," but with a new job title and the added pressure of having to be a "rainmaker"—that is, bring in new business for the firm.

Not only is the carrot further away for young associates, it's a spoiled carrot, at that. Somewhere toward the end of my first year at the firm, I had gleaned enough insights into senior attorneys' personal lives to know that I didn't want to follow in their footsteps. Simply put, few of them seemed happy. In fact, having succumbed to the pressures of practice over the years, most seemed bitter, frustrated, impatient, and even hostile. I often sensed this even from passing senior attorneys in the office halls, where the tension on even an average day could be palpable.

I began to realize that I disliked most aspects of my job, and, even worse, that I would never find it very fulfilling or rewarding. Although I realized that my salary and control over cases would increase if I stayed, I knew that the essential nature of my job would always remain the same, even if I someday did make partner.

At the same time, I found that most of my colleagues and friends in other top firms were having similar doubts about their careers. Our firms seemed to differ in name only; as associates, we were fungible commodities no matter where we worked. The proverbial carrot simply disappeared for me, and along with it, my old incentive to work hard and remain dedicated. I began to perceive my job as a long, narrow passageway that ultimately dead-ended. The only thing that kept me working hard was my pride in producing high quality work. The ultimate reward in producing that work was gone.

Once my goal of partnership crumbled, I began to resent virtually every facet of my work. I even resented the salary, hard as that may be to believe, considering I was making almost $100,000 a year. But here's why I was resentful. That salary was the underlying reason the firm felt it could squeeze so many painfully long hours out of me. But I began to realize that there wasn't any economic justification for me putting in extra hours, because I didn't get paid for them. In this way, young associates *are* different from doctors, dentists, stockbrokers, real estate agents, and other professionals. All of the others at least have the potential to earn more if they work harder or longer. Doctors and dentists, for instance, might get an extra $60 or so if they see an extra patient at the end of the day. And stockbrokers often earn additional commissions if they put in the time to research companies and then contact their clients about a good investment. But I couldn't meaningfully correlate the extra hours I spent with my salary. Even my year-end bonus was unlikely to reflect any extra effort I put in.

My attitude about my salary soured even more when I realized that, in spite of the amount of money I was receiving, it wasn't so hot after all when I compared it to the amount of work I was doing in return for it. My colleagues and I often joked that, despite our high salaries and 20 years' of education, we were probably earning minimum wage for the high number of hours we worked. It was a joke with an edge. We often felt as though we were being paid just enough to keep us from quitting.

In fact, I began to wonder if my salary shackled me to my firm. This is a phenomenon called "golden handcuffs," and it refers to the exceptionally high salary large firms pay, and the effect it has on associates. If you try to jump ship as a junior associate to a job you'd prefer in a government agency, company, or small to medium-sized firm, your pay cut will probably be between $15,000 and $60,000. That's a pay *cut*. This economic disincentive to leave grows into an addiction for many attorneys, who find that that addiction grows stronger with each year and each salary increase.

I determined not to let the "golden handcuffs" trap me, even though the salary had been one of the things that seemed most attractive to me when I joined the firm. After 3 years of scrimping in law school, I had thoroughly enjoyed the prospect of spending my substantial income on a lifestyle I had envisioned and worked so hard to obtain. I bought a nice condominium, fitted it out with expensive furniture, bought state-of-the-art stereo equipment and a beautiful Porsche. At first, owning these things felt like an achievement for me, a signal to myself and to the world that I was successful. But as I grew disenchanted with my job, my attitude towards my possessions changed. I realized that I had hardly any time to enjoy them, and even when I did, I didn't enjoy them nearly as much as I thought I would. The fact is, none of my possessions could fill the voids I felt in my life. I might as well have thrown all of them into a black hole. Ironically, by the time I decided to leave the firm, I was actually eager to sell most of my once-coveted possessions, recognizing them for what they were: the trappings of an unhealthy, stressful lifestyle that very nearly ate me alive.

May 26

Today I resigned.

In retrospect, only the timing wasn't planned. I had actually resolved to leave the law months ago, when I could no longer think of a reason to stay. I wanted to act quickly to cut my losses, but my job never allowed me sufficient time to explore other career opportunities. I finally decided a few days ago to wait another month or so, and then give my 2 weeks' notice in order to minimize my time as a "lame duck" employee receiving the worst assignments. Last night, though, I realized I'd have to come clean sooner than I thought, out of fairness to both Brad and my client, General Utilities.

The chain of events leading up to this realization began yesterday afternoon, when Brad flew into Memphis airport for several meetings at the utility's headquarters. Brad met with the general counsel until the early evening and then joined several of us working in some unused cubicles. I was working on a witness preparation outline when Brad and a paralegal sat down at the computer in the cubicle opposite mine and began preparing a work schedule for the next 4 months. A few days ago, the government informed us that it would be taking testimony from about 20 witnesses and that it had already selected tentative dates for the witnesses. With the government's list in hand, Brad and the paralegal prepared a calendar showing each scheduled day of testimony, the prep days for each witness, and the lawyers responsible for prepping each witness. I'm not sure how may times I heard my name over the next hour or so as they discussed the schedule, but I knew it was too many. I confirmed my suspicions after Brad got up and left: my name was plastered all over that calendar.

Last night, with the calendar in mind, I thought hard about whether I should wait to give my notice, and even talked it out with friends. Despite my desire to wait, I felt professionally obligated to tell Brad that I was planning to leave the firm. I had known all along my replacement would need a few weeks to learn the complex facts of this case, but the government's proposed tentative testimony dates created a deadline by which someone would have to replace me. I reluctantly admitted to myself that it wouldn't be fair to my client or Brad if my sudden departure impaired the witness preparation process during a government investigation. I decided to tell Brad today, since I wasn't expecting to see him again for another week or so.

I woke up groggy and with a nervous stomach, having slept poorly in anticipation of my conversation with Brad. My doubts about quitting the law despite my personal and financial investment began to intensify as the time to take action approached. My friends, family, and colleagues had told me repeatedly that I was making the right decision, but I knew that, in the end, the decision was mine alone to make. I knew they meant well, but I couldn't help but wonder if they would have followed their own advice if they had been in my shoes.

I waited nervously for an opportunity to speak privately with Brad as we worked busily in the same cubicle-filled area we occupied last night. I finally got my chance about 10 o'clock this morning, when Brad got off a long telephone call. I asked him to step into an empty office and closed the door behind us as he sat down at a small circular table. I decided to be brief since he was busy and I was feeling queasy.

"I've given this a lot of thought," I said cautiously, "and I'm leaving the firm."

He shot back, "Shut up and stop being silly."

I dug in my heels and insisted I was serious. He assured me I was making a mistake, and told me I was abandoning a successful and promising future with the firm. I didn't want to argue with him, though, and merely explained that I had to leave the law for awhile before I'd again be able to practice it zealously.

He soon realized I'd made up my mind, and asked, "When are you leaving?"

"Six weeks."

For better or worse, it was done. I was still nervous, but I felt different as I walked out of that office. I had taken the first and single most important step in regaining control of my life.

I was free.

EPILOGUE

After leaving his firm, Bill Keates moved to San Francisco in search of a new life. He joined a boutique consulting firm as a management consultant to major financial services companies.

He says, "Despite the daily stresses in my life now, I'm happier than I ever was as an attorney."

Incidentally, he traded in the Porsche for a Ford Explorer.

PUBLISHED SOURCES

American Bar Association. *The Report of At The Breaking Point: A National Conference on The Emerging Crisis in the Quality of Lawyers' Health and Lives—Its Impact on Law Firms and Client Services. Virginia: American Bar Association [1991]*.

American Bar Association, Young Lawyers Division. *The State of the Legal Profession, 1990* (Executive Summary), 1990.

Benjamin, G.; Andrew H.; Darling, Elaine J.; and Sales, Bruce. "The Prevalence of Depression, Alcohol Abuse and Cocaine Abuse Among United States Lawyers." *International Journal of Law and Psychiatry* 13 (Summer 1990):233–246.

Black, Henry Campbell. *Black's Law Dictionary*, Abridged 5th ed., St. Paul: West Publishing Co., 1983.

Coleman, Francis T. "Rethinking Personnel Strategies." *Washington Lawyer*, January/February 1995, pp. 32–40.

Determan, Sara-Ann. "Substance Abuse: Not To Be Denied." *The Washington Lawyer*, March-April 1991, pp. 8–9.

Edelstein, David R. "Practicing Law: A Challenge To Your Mental Health." *CBA Record*, June 1994, pp. 24–29.

Edwards, Harry T. "The Growing Disjunction Between Legal Education and the Legal Profession." *Michigan Law Journal* 1991.

Fitzpatrick, James F., "Legal Future Shock: The Role of Large Law Firms by the End of the Century." *Indiana Law Journal* 64 (Summer 1989):461–71.

Gebaide, Eric F. "Summer Associate Programs: It Pays to Advertise," *Law Practice Management*, March 1990, pp. 45–52.

Hengstler, Gary A. "Vox Populi; The Public Perception of Lawyers: ABA Poll." *ABA Journal*, September 1993, pp. 60–65.

Hickey, Mary C. "Attorney Alcoholism." *Washington Lawyer*, March-April 1990, pp. 35–42.

Ide, R. William III. "What the ABA Plans to Do," *ABA Journal*, September 1993, p. 65.

Itkin, Don. "Are You a Fish In a Bird's Nest?" *Wisconsin Lawyer*, July 1992, pp. 12–15; 56.

Kunz, Christina L.; Schmedemann, Deborah A; Erlinder, C. Peter; Downs, Matthew P.; and Bateson, Ann L. *The Process of Legal Research*, 2nd ed. Boston: Little, Brown & Company, 1989.

Lefer, Gary L. "Attorneys Are Most Severely Stressed Groups." *New York Law Journal*, 20 September 1986, p. 23.

Lempinen, Edward W. "Make Mine Beluga." *Student Lawyer*, February 1990, pp. 4–7.

Lhamon, Judith A. "Providing Students With Data." *National Law Journal*, 30 April 1990, p. 22.

Lyons, James. "It's Not A Wonderful Situation." *Forbes*, February 4, 1991, pp. 90–92.

Mestel, Lynn. "Associates Address Problems on the Road to Partnership," *New York Law Journal*, 9 March 1992, sec. S, p. S-1.

Myers, Ken. "The Interviews May Be Grueling, But Students Don't Miss Class." *National Law Journal*, 10 September 1990, p. 4.

National Association for Law Placement. *Directory of Legal Employers*. Washington, DC: National Association for Law Placement, 1994.

Rehnquist, William H. "The Legal Profession Today." *Indiana Law Journal* 62 (Spring 1987):151–57.

Saltzman, Amy. "Reinventing Partnership." *U.S. News & World Report*, 7 May 1990, pp. 67–70.

Samborn, Randall. "Anti-Lawyer Attitude Up." *National Law Journal*, 9 August 1993, p. 1.

Samborn, Randall. "Firms Slowly Come to Grips With Addiction." *National Law Journal*, 10 December 1990, p. 1.

Sansing, John. "First, Kill All The Lawyers." *Washingtonian*, November 1990, pp. 132–42.

Sansing, John. "Mommas, Don't Let Your Babies Grow Up to Be Lawyers," *Washingtonian*, November 1990, pp. 136–37.

Santangelo, Charles J.; and Morrison, Donald W. "Alcohol Abuse on the Rise Among Lawyers: Stress at Work Takes Its Toll." *New York Law Journal*, 5 April 1993, p. 5.

Sells, Benjamin. "To Cope or Quit Isn't The Only Choice." *Los Angeles Daily Journal*, 23 December 1993.

Shapo, Helene S.; Walter, Marilyn R.; and Fajans, Elizabeth. *Writing and Analysis in the Law*. Westbury, NY: The Foundation Press, Inc., 1989.

Stevens, Amy. "Why Lawyers Are Depressed, Anxious, Bored Insomniacs." *Wall Street Journal*. 13 June 1995, p. B1.

Sullivan, Teresa. "More 'Feedback' Needed By Young Lawyers: Panel." *Chicago Daily Law Bulletin*, 6 April 1990, p. 2.

STARTING SALARIES FOR NEW ASSOCIATES AT THE 250 LARGEST LAW FIRMS IN AMERICA

(Source: *The National Law Journal,* October 9, 1995. Reprinted with the permission of *The National Law Journal.* Copyright 1996, *The New York Law Publishing Company.*)

Note: The NLJ survey was accompanied by pages of footnotes, highlighting specifics about each firm's starting salaries. Therefore, the figures given here provide only a ballpark idea of what the large firms pay their new associates.

1. Baker & McKenzie	$70,000
2. Skadden, Arps, Slate, Meagher & Flom	$85,000
3. Jones, Day, Reavis & Pogue	$74,000–83,000
4. Morgan, Lewis & Bockius	$70,000
5. Latham & Watkins	$74,000–82,333
6. Gibson, Dunn & Crutcher	$80,000–85,000
7. Sidley & Austin	$70,000
8. Mayer, Brown & Platt	$72,500–85,000
9. Fulbright & Jaworski	$62,200–83,000
10. White & Case	$85,000
11. Shearman & Sterling	$86,000
12. Weil, Gotshal & Manges	$83,000
13. Akin, Gump, Strauss, Hauer & Feld	$57,000–66,000
14. McDermott, Will & Emery	$70,000
15. O'Melveny & Myers	$80,300
16. Vinson & Elkins	$61,500
17. Morrison &Foerster	$67,000–71,000
18. Pillsbury, Madison & Sutro	$67,000–71,000

19. LeBoeuf, Lamb, Greene & MacRae — $85,000
20. Bryan Cave — $56,000–81,000
21. Winston & Strawn — $70,000–83,000
22. Cleary, Gottlieb, Steen & Hamilton — $83,000
23. Kirkland & Ellis — $66,000–84,000
24. Foley & Lardner — $55,000–72,000
25. Hunton & Williams — $57,000–77,000
26. Baker & Hostetler — $74,000
27. Sonnenschein Nath & Rosenthal — $70,000
28. Simpson Thacher & Bartlett — $87,000
29. Hogan & Hartson — $72,000
30. Proskauer Rose Goetz & Mendelsohn — $85,000
31. Davis Polk & Wardwell — $87,000
32. Baker & Botts — $62,000–83,000
33. Rogers & Wells — $86,000
34. Holland & Knight — $47,000–76,000
35. Brobeck, Phleger & Harrison — $70,000
36. Kirkpatrick & Lockhart — $66,000–93,000
37. Sullivan & Cromwell — $86,500
38. Fried, Frank, Harris, Shriver & Jacobson — $86,000
39. Paul, Hastings, Janofsky & Walker — $75,000
40. Wilson, Eloser, Moskowitz, Edelman & Dicker — $54,000
41. McGuire, Woods, Battle & Booths — $60,000–71,000
42. Dewey Ballantine — $86,000
43. Jenner & Block — $70,000
44. Willkie Farr & Gallagher — $90,000
45. Dorsey & Whitney — $58,000
46. Milbank, Tweed Hadley & McCloy — $85,000
47. Squire, Sanders & Dempsey — $66,000–76,000
48. Reed Smith Shaw & McClay — $71,050
49. Arnold & Porter — $72,000
50. Dechert Price & Rhoads — $61,000–83,000
51. Hinshaw & Culbertson — N/A
52. Kaye, Scholer, Fierman, Hays & Handler — $85,000
53. Debevoise & Plimpton — $86,000
54. King & Spalding — $60,000–82,000
55. Paul, Weiss, Rifkind, Wharton & Garrison — $83,000

56. Cravath, Swaine & Moore	$85,000
57. Katten Muchin & Zavis	$72,000
58. Perkins Coie	$56,333–79, 333
59. Seyfarth, Shaw, Fairweather & Geraldson	$75,500
60. Thompson, Hine & Flory	$59,000–66,000
61. Lord, Bissell & Brook	$70,000
62. Orrick, Herrington & Sutcliffe	$60,000–85,000
63. Chadbourne & Parke	$85,000
64. Howrey & Simon	$70,000
65. Ropes & Gray	$73,000
66. Goudert Brothers	$83,000
67. Arter & Hadden	$64,000
68. Piper & Marbury	$60,000
69. Alston & Bird	$60,000
70. Goodwin, Procter & Hoar	$73,000
71. Kelley Drye & Warren	$85,000
72. Graham & James	$73,000
73. Heller, Ehrman, White & McAuliffe	$67,000
74. Covington & Burling	$72,000
75. Stroock & Stroock & Lavan	$85,000
76. Shaw, Pittman, Potts & Trowbridge	$72,000
77. Quarles & Brady	$66,000
78. Brown & Wood	$83,000
79. Faegre & Benson	$58,000
80. Vorys, Sater, Seymour and Pease	$64,000
81. Sutherland, Asbill & Brennan	$60,000–82,000
82. Pepper, Hamiton & Scheetz	$55,000–72,000
83. Ballard Spahr Andrews & Ingersoll	$68,500
84. McKenna & Cuneo	$56,000–72,000
85. Cadwalader, Wickersham & Taft	$83,000
86. Davis Wright Tremaine	$51,000
87. Hale and Dorr	$73,000
88. Lane Powell Spears Lubersky	$51,000
89. Keck, Mahin & Gate	$79,000–82,500
90. Venable, Baetjer and Howard	$57,000–65,000
91. Wilson Sonsini Goodrich & Rosati	$72,000
92. Gray Cary Ware & Freidenrich	$67,000–71,000

93. Nixon, Hargrave, Devans & Doyle	$57,000–84,000
94. Buchanan Ingersoll	$66,000
95. Mudge Rose Guthrie Alexander & Ferdon	$85,000
96. Sedwick, Detert, Moran & Arnold	N/A
97. Cooley, Godward Castro Huddleson & Tatum	$68,000–71,000
98. Haynes and Boone	$64,209–65,209
99. Littler, Mendelson, Fastiff, Tichy & Mathiason	$60,000-71,000
100. Stoel Rives	$50,000
101. Winthrop, Stimson, Putnam & Roberts	$86,000
102. Epstein Becker & Green	$74,000
103. Popham, Haik, Schnobrich & Laufman	$58,000
104. Dickinson, Wright, Moon, Van Dusen & Freeman	$60,000
105. McCutchen, Doyle, Brown & Enersen	$68,000–70,000
106. Hughes Hubbard & Reed	$83,000
107. Greenberg, Traurig	$63,000
108. Andrews & Kurth	$60,000–87,000
109. Rosenman & Colin	$82,000
110. Wilmer, Cutler & Pickering	$72,000
111. Snell & Wilmer	$46,000–70,000
112. Miller, Canfield, Paddock and Stone	$65,000
113. Shook, Hardy & Bacon	$58,500
114. Porter, Wright, Morris & Arthur	$60,000–62,000
115. Robins, Kaplan, Miller & Ciresi	$56,000
116. Dykema Gossett	$60,000
117. Jenkens & Gilchrist	$55,000
118. Powell, Goldstein, Frazer & Murphy	$60,000
119. Arent Fox Kintner Plotkin & Kahn	$73,000
120. Day, Berry & Howard	$61,000–71,000
121. Blank, Rome, Comisky & McCauley	$60,000
122. Cahill Gordon & Reindel	$83,000
123. Gardner, Carton & Douglas	$75,300
124. Loeb and Loeb	$72,000–80,000
125. Sheppard, Mullin, Richter & Hampton	$75,000
126. Eckert Seamans Cherin & Mellott	$62,800

127. Kutak Rock	$54,000–65,000
128. Rudnick & Wolfe	$68,000
129. Crowell & Moring	$72,000
130. Nelson Mullins Riley & Scarborough	$55,000–65,000
131. Bingham, Dana & Gould	$73,000
132. Whitman Breed Abbott & Morgan	$83,000
133. Honigman Miller Schwartz and Cohn	$60,000–75,000
134. Bracewell & Patterson	$62,000–69,000
135. Duane, Morris & Heckscher	$68,000
136. Preston Gates & Ellis	$50,000
137. Oppenheimer Wolff & Donnelly	$57,000
138. Kilpatrick & Cody	$60,000
139. Steptoe & Johnson	$72,000
140. Anderson Kill Olick & Oshinsky	$83,000
141. Bogle & Gates	$55,750
142. Cozen and O'Connor	$60,000
143. Mintz, Levin, Cohn, Ferris, Glovsky & Popeo	$72,000
144. Patton Boggs	$75,500
145. Altheimer & Gray	$70,000
146. Schiff Hardin & Waite	$77,360
147. Jackson, Lewis, Schnitzler & Krupman	$65,000
148. Gardere & Wynne	$56,000
149. Holland & Hart	$52,000
150. Thompson & Knight	$61,000
151. Drinker Biddle & Reath	$63,000
152. Chapman and Cutler	$70,000
153. Baker & Daniels	$61,000
154. Marshall, Dennehey, Warner, Coleman & Goggin	$40,000
155. Ross & Hardies	$67,000
156. Morrison, Mahoney & Miller	N/A
157. Strasburger & Price	$61,000
158. McCarter & Eglish	$65,000
159. Dinsmore & Shohl	$60,000
160. Crosby, Heafey, Roach & May	$65,000–70,000
161. Phelps Dunbar	$45,000–54,000
162. Baker, Donelson, Bearman & Caldwell	$50,000–52,000

163. Troutman Sanders	$60,000
164. Locke Purnell Rain Harrell	$58,000
165. Michael, Best & Friedrich	$65,000
166. Thompson & Mitchell	$56,000
167. Wiley, Rein & Fielding	$78,000
168. Schulte, Roth & Zabel	$83,000
169. Ice Miller Donadio & Ryan	$63,000
170. Mendes & Mount	N/A
171. Schnader, Harrison, Segal & Lewis	$63,000
172. Holme Roberts & Owen	$52,000
173. Lewis, D'Amato, Brisbois & Bisgaard	$56,000
174. Thelen, Marrin, Johnson & Bridges	$65,000
175. Reid & Priest	$83,000
176. Barnes & Thornburg	$63,000
177. Miles & Stockbridge	$58,000–65,000
178. Hopkins & Sutter	$70,000
179. Steel Hector & Davis	$57,500
180. Wyatt, Tarrant & Combs	$51,500
181. Ropers, Majeski, Kohn & Bentley	$50,000
182. Womble Carlyle Sandridge & Rice	$57,000
183. Wolf, Block, Schorr & Solis-Cohen	$68,000
184. Bell, Boyd & Lloyd	$70,000
185. Choate, Hall & Stewart	$70,000
186. Rivkin, Radler & Kremer	$50,000
187. Jackson & Walker	$59,000–59,500
188. Winstead Sechrest & Minick	$60,000
189. Blackwell Sanders Matheny Weary & Lombardi	$57,500
190. Manatt, Phelps & Phillips	$70,000
191. Vedder, Price, Kaufman & Kammholz	$70,000
192. Armstrong, Teasdale, Schlafly & Davis	$56,000
193. Palmer & Dodge	$73,000
194. Testa, Hurwitz & Thibeault	$74,000
195. White and Williams	$60,000
196. Wildman, Harrold, Allen & Dixon	$68,000
197. Pennie & Edmonds	$83,000
198. Dickstein, Shapiro & Morin	$70,000

199. Edwards & Angell $55,000
200. Irell & Manella $70,000
201. Robinson & Cole $57,000–60,000
202. Pitney, Hardin, Kipp & Szuch $62,000–65,500
203. Foley, Hoag & Eliot $73,000
204. Frost & Jacobs $60,000
205. Vernier, Lupfert, Bernhard, McPherson
    & Hand $70,000
206. Curtis, Mallet-Prevost, Colt & Moble $83,000
207. Liddell, Sapp, Zivley, Hill & LaBoon $62,500
208. Saul, Ewing, Remick & Saul $62,500
209. Hodgson, Russ, Andrews, Woods & Goodyear $50,000
210. Bond, Schoeneck & King $53,000
211. Jacoby & Meyers N/A
212. Riker, Danzig, Scherer, Hyland & Perretti $64,000
213. Calfee, Halter & Griswold $67,500
214. Finnegan, Henderson, Farabow, Garrett
    & Dunner $80,000
215. Haight, Brown & Bonesteel $55,000–61,000
216. Butzel Long $60,000
217. Hughes & Luce $60,000
218. Smith Helms Mulliss & Moore $56,500
219. Taft, Stettinius & Hollister $62,000
220. Carlton, Fields, Ward, Emmanuel, Smith
    & Cutler $54,000–58,000
221. Montgomery McCracken Walker & Rhoads $60,000
222. Foster, Pepper & Shefelman $54,000
223. Harris Beach & Wilcox $45,000
224. McGlinchey Stafford Lang $52,000
225. Ruden Barnett McClosky Smith Schuster Russel $55,000
226. Bronson, Bronson & McKinnon $65,000
227. Cummings & Lockwood $60,000
228. Williams & Connolly $77,500
229. Jackson & Kelly $50,500
230. Kramer, Levin, Laftalis, Nessen, Kamin
    & Frankel $83,000
231. Morrison & Hecker $55,500

232. Tacher Proffitt & Wood — $82,000
233. Lewis, Rice & Fingersh — $56,000
234. Phillips, Lytle, Hitchcock, Blaine & Huber — $50,000
235. Benesch, Friedlander, Coplan & Aronoff — $64,000
236. Clausen, Miller — N/A
237. Sullivan & Worcester — $68,000
238. Lowenstein, Sandler, , Kohl, Fisher & Boylan — $70,000
239. Sills Cummis Zuckerman Radin Tischman
Epstein & Gross — $65,500
240. Warner Norcross & Judd — $55,000
241. Luce, Forward, Hamilton & Scripps — $72,583
242. Post & Schell — N/A
243. Querry & Harrow — $50,000
244. Adams and Reese — $48,000
245. Fowler, White, Gillen, Boggs, Villareal
& Banker — $54,000
246. Ober, Kaler, Grimes & Shriver — $54,000
247. Stites & Harrison — $43,000
248. Swidler & Berlin — $77,000
249. Briggs and Morgan — $58,000
250. Husch & Eppenberger — $55,000